3A

SPLIT EDITION

LIVE BEAT

STUDENTS' BOOK

Liz Kilbey • Ingrid Freebairn • Jonathan Bygrave • Judy Copage

Pearson Education Limited,
Edinburgh Gate, Harlow
Essex, CM20 2JE, England
and Associated Companies throughout the world

ww.pearsonelt.com

First published 2015

ISBN 978-1- 292-10196-5

Set in Set in Helvetica Neue LTD Std 55 Roman 10/14 pt

Photo Acknowledgements

The publisher would like to thank the following for their kind permission
to reproduce their photographs:

(Key: b-bottom; c-centre; l-left; r-right; t-top)

Alamy Images: Catchlight Visual Services 28b, Jim Forrest 12tr, Greg
Balfour Evans 44b, Steven Harrison 41br, i love images 51, Janine
Wiedel Photolibrary 12bl, Justin Kasez 12z 32bl, moodboard 6cr, one-
image photography 19bl, Realimage 40cr, RMIreland 40tr, Marmaduke
St. John

24cr, The Photolibrary Wales 19tl, Travelshots.com / Peter Phipp 32br,
39bl, Washington Stock Photo 28tr; **BananaStock:** 24tr; **Corbis:** Demotix
/ Peter Stanley 18br, Image Source 46b, Lived in Images / Douglas Keister
6br; **DK Images:** Chris Stowers 38br; **Fotolia.com:** Kwokfai 39tc,
photomic 39bc, Peggy Stein 39br, Syda Productions 31tr; **Getty Images:**
Jeff J Mitchell 48; **Pearson Education Ltd:** Gareth Boden 4, 6t, 8tr, 10,
11t, 11bl, 11br, 14, 22, 35, 42cl, 44tl, 44tr, 46t, Naki Kouyioumtzis 39tl,
Sozaijiten 36tr, 36cr, 36b, Tudor Photography 49; © **Rough Guides:**
Suzanne Porter 8b; **Shutterstock.com:** Bikeworldtravel 33, Sebastien
Burel 42b, Shae Cardenas 19cl, Honza Hruby 45, Neil Mitchell 32tr;
SuperStock: Sheltered Images 6bl; **The Kobal Collection:** Columbia /
Marvel 16cr, New Line Cinema 16tr, 16br

Cover images: *Front:* **Shutterstock.com:** Rido

All other images © Pearson Education

Every effort has been made to trace the copyright holders and we
apologise in advance for any unintentional omissions. We would be
pleased to insert the appropriate acknowledgement in any subsequent
edition of this publication.

Special thanks to the following for their help during location photography:

Planet Clothing, Hitchin; Shephalbury Sports Academy, Stevenage; Tech
Trade-In, Hitchin

Illustration Acknowledgements

David Banks page; Adrian Barclay (Beehive Illustration); Kathy
Baxendale; Paco Cavero (Sylvie Poggio); Stephen Elford; Kevin
Hopgood; Richard Jones (Beehive Illustration); Wes Lowe (Beehive
Illustration); David Shenton; Eric Smith (KJA); Roger Wade Walker
(Beehive Illustration); Ian West (Beehive Illustration); Tony Wilkins

Contents

WELCOME

Emma: Hi, Luke. Hi, Jodie. What **are** you **doing** here?

Luke: Hi, Emma. We**'re applying** for the free month. Are you a member?

Emma: Yes, I **play** badminton here every week – but I'm not very good.

Jodie: Don't listen to her. She's brilliant.

Luke: Look, that's the new boy in my class. He's American.

Emma: What's he like?

Luke: He **seems** OK, quite friendly and easy-going. Oh cool, he**'s coming** in ... Hi, Martin!

Martin: Hi, er ... sorry, I **don't remember** ...

Luke: Luke.

Jodie: I'm his sister, Jodie, and this is Emma.

Martin: Hi, nice to meet you. **Do** you **live** near here?

Luke: Not far away. What about you?

Martin: We**'re renting** an apartment round the corner. My dad's a teacher. We're only here for a year.

Jodie: Great. Welcome to London!

1 Listen and read. Name the people in the photo.

A – Jodie

2 Complete with *Luke, Jodie, Emma* or *Martin*.

1 *Emma* is a member of the sports club.
2 ___ is American.
3 ___ and ___ are in the same class at school.
4 ___ is ___'s brother.
5 ___'s dad is a teacher.

Personality adjectives

3 Look at the personality adjectives from the Word bank on page 56. Then write the words in the correct lists. Which words could go in both lists?

🙂	🙁
clever	

4 **In pairs, describe the people using the adjectives in Exercise 3. Take turns to ask and answer.**

1 Ben gets good marks at school.
   A: What's Ben like?
   B: He's clever. He gets good marks at school.
2 Alex and Shaun like meeting people.
3 Amy doesn't like spending money.
4 Tom always makes people laugh.
5 Rosa likes helping people.
6 Jack always gets up late and doesn't work very hard.
7 Kate never says 'please' or 'thank you'.
8 Tim loves giving presents to his friends and family.

Present simple and present continuous

Name the tenses
1 What **are** you **doing** here?
2 I **play** badminton here every week.
3 He **seems** OK.
4 **I don't remember**.
5 We**'re renting** an apartment.

Stative verbs
We don't normally use these verbs in the continuous: *be, believe, forget, hate, hear, hope, know, like, love, mean, need, prefer, remember, see, seem, sound, understand, want*

Complete the rules.

We use the ¹___ tense for permanent situations and routines.
We use the ²___ tense for activities which are happening at or around the time of speaking.

5 **Choose the correct options.**

1 Sorry, I don't remember / 'm not remembering your name.
2 Hi! Where **do you go** / **are you going**?
3 Ssh! We **watch** / **'re watching** TV.
4 Jack **always sits** / **'s always sitting** at the back of the class.
5 We **study** / **'re studying** Shakespeare this term.
6 May **doesn't like** / **isn't liking** loud music.

6 **Complete the sentences with the present simple or present continuous form of the verbs.**

1 Luke, Jodie and Emma *live* (live) in London. Martin ___ (stay) in London for a year.
2 My sister ___ (love) adventure stories. At the moment she ___ (read) *The Hunger Games*.
3 I ___ (not want) to go out now – it ___ (rain).
4 What's funny? Why ___ (you laugh)? I ___ (not understand).
5 ___ (you enjoy) the party? I ___ (hope) so!
6 My mum ___ (call) me. She ___ (wait) for me downstairs.

7a **Take turns to talk about somebody in your family. Your partner takes notes.**

• What's he/she like?
• What does he/she do every day?
• What does he/she usually do at the weekend?
• What's he/she doing at the moment? (Guess!)
My brother's clever, but he's really lazy. He goes to this school. At the weekend he plays a lot of computer games. At the moment, he's having a Maths lesson.

b **Now write about the person your partner described.**

Anna's brother is clever, but …

1 🎧 **Listen and read. What does Martin like about his London home?**

Martin:	I've got some photos here – look, this is my house in California.
Jodie:	Wow, it looks great! What about inside? Have you got any more photos?
Martin:	Not on my phone. It's quite big inside, but there are only three bedrooms.
Jodie:	Are all the rooms on one floor?
Martin:	Yes, there aren't any stairs, but there is a small loft.
Jodie:	Cool, I love lofts!
Martin:	Not this one! It's dark and there's no window. There's just some old furniture up there.
Jodie:	Well, now you're in a flat on the 5th floor. That's a big change.
Martin:	Yes, it's different … but I like it. It's got a balcony! We haven't got one back home.
Jodie:	But you've got a garden there. Have you got a swimming pool?
Martin:	No, there isn't any space. But it doesn't matter, there's a pool next door!

2 **Look at the photos (1–3). Which one is Martin's house?**

My Photos   **Upload**

1

2

3

House and furniture

3a Put the words from the box into the correct lists.

> • balcony • bathroom • bedroom • bookcase • carpet
> • ceiling • cooker • dishwasher • floor • fridge • hall
> • kitchen • lamp • mirror • sink • wall

Rooms: *bathroom, …* **Fittings:** *cooker, …*
Parts of a house: *balcony, …* **Furniture:** *bookcase, …*

b Work in pairs. Add more words to the lists, then check the Word bank on page 56.

4 Look at the picture for one minute, then cover it. How many things can you remember? Tell your partner.

a kitchen, a …

Countable and uncountable nouns with *some, any, a/an* and *no*

Countable		Uncountable
Affirmative		
It's got **a** balcony. There is **a** loft.	I've got **some** photos. There are **some** photos.	There's **some** old furniture. It's got **some** old furniture.
Negative		
There isn't **a** window. There's **no** window.	There aren't **any** stairs. There are **no** stairs.	There isn't **any** space. There is **no** space.
Questions		
Have you got **a** swimming pool?	Have you got **any** photos?	Is there **any** furniture?

> **Note**
> Uncountable nouns do not have a plural form.

5 Complete the sentences with *some, any, a/an* or *no*.

1 There's <u>a</u> big fridge in the kitchen but there isn't ___ food in it!
2 There's ___ rubbish on the floor. Have you got ___ wastepaper bin?
3 Sorry, you can't sit here, there's ___ space – but there are ___ chairs over there.
4 I want to buy ___ chocolate. Have you got ___ money?
5 Yes, we've got ___ garden, but I'm afraid there aren't ___ flowers – only ___ grass.
6 There's ___ old bookcase in the hall with ___ mirror above it.

6 Match questions (1–6) to answers (a–f). Then complete them with *some, any, a/an* or *no*.

1 – b

1 Have you got <u>*any*</u> homework tonight?
2 Is there ___ food in the fridge?
3 Is there ___ furniture in the new classroom?
4 Has Joe got ___ new bike?
5 Have you got ___ good CDs?
6 Is there ___ computer in that classroom?

a) Not really, but I've got ___ cool music on my phone.
b) Yes, but I haven't got <u>*any*</u> time to do it!
c) Yes, there's ___ cheese and ___ box of eggs.
d) Yes, there are ___ chairs, but there are ___ desks.
e) Yes, but there's ___ printer.
f) No, he's got ___ old one.

7 Work in pairs. Take turns to describe your ideal bedroom or living room. Ask and answer questions about the room.

A: My ideal living room has got a big TV on one of the walls.
B: What about furniture? Is there a big sofa?

C

1 🎧 **Read Martin's blog. What does his father teach?**

My BLOG

Home   About   BLOG   Contact

Sept 5th

It was raining when we landed in London and after California it felt COLD. Our apartment isn't bad. The best thing is, Jamie and I have got our own rooms. When we arrived I wanted to go online straightaway, but there was no connection. This morning an engineer came … and here I am. Now what????

Sept 10th

I started school on Monday (it's a bit strange but OK) and I'm feeling more at home now. I went to the local sports centre on Saturday. A guy called Luke was there (he's in my new class), with his sister and her friend. While we were talking we discovered something embarrassing – the friend (her name's Emma) is in my dad's Science class, but luckily not at my school!

Sept 17th

Luke and I went sightseeing at the weekend and we saw Buckingham Palace. Lots of police officers and journalists were waiting outside while we were queuing – I think they were expecting someone important (they weren't waiting for us!).

2 **Answer true (T), false (F) or doesn't say (DS).**

1 Martin is from California. *T*

2 His apartment does not have an internet connection.

3 He's beginning to like his new home.

4 His father teaches Emma.

5 They visited several famous places in London.

Jobs

3a Find three jobs in the blog. Put them into the correct columns.

-er	-or	-ist	-ian	other
engineer				

b Now complete the jobs and add them to the table, then check the Word bank on page 56.

1 act*or*
2 art_
3 build_
4 dent_
5 detect_
6 direct_
7 doct_
8 electric_
9 farm_
10 firefight_
11 mod_
12 music_
13 reception_
14 shop assist_

4 Answer the questions. Sometimes there is more than one answer. Then check the Word bank on page 56.

Who …
1 fights fires? *a firefighter*
2 works with make-up?
3 cuts hair?
4 teaches skiing?
5 works with cars?
6 flies planes?
7 looks after the home?
8 cooks food?
9 serves food?
10 looks after animals?

Past simple and past continuous

Time markers: *when, while*

Name the tenses (1–9).

It ¹**was raining** when we ²**landed** in London.
When we ³**arrived** I ⁴**wanted** to go online.
While ⁵**we were talking**, we ⁶**discovered** something embarrassing.
Lots of police officers and journalists ⁷**were waiting** outside while we ⁸**were queuing**.
They ⁹**weren't waiting** for us!

Complete the rules.

We often use …
the ¹⁰___ tense to describe completed actions.
the ¹¹___ tense to describe actions that continued for some time in the past.
the word ¹²___ to introduce clauses in the past simple.
the word ¹³___ to introduce clauses in the past continuous.

5 Choose the correct options. Then complete the sentences with the correct form of the verbs.

1 Sam was cycling home **when** / while the police officer *stopped* (stop) him.
2 **When / While** the shop assistant opened the doors, a lot of customers ___ (wait) outside.
3 What was Jill doing **when / while** you ___ (see) her?
4 Dan ___ (play) football **when / while** he fell and hurt his leg.
5 I ___ (drop) my phone **when / while** I was walking home.
6 **When / While** the teacher ___ (talk), the students were taking notes.

6 Complete the next part of Martin's blog with the correct form of the verbs.

Sept 25ᵗʰ

Luke and I were at the sports centre yesterday. We ¹*didn't want* (not want) to do the same things. I ²___ (go) to the gym. While I ³___ (work) hard on the rowing machine, Luke ⁴___ (swim) lengths – he's a really good swimmer. After that we ⁵___ (decide) to go to the café. When we ⁶___ (walk) in, Jodie and Emma ⁷___ (sit) there, so we ⁸___ (join) them. While we ⁹___ (talk), I ¹⁰___ (ask) Emma about my dad. She ¹¹___ (say) he's quite a cool teacher! That's hard to believe.

7 Talk about your family. Use the prompts and *when* or *while*.

What were they doing when/while you …
• got home yesterday?
• went to bed last night?
• were having breakfast?
• left home this morning?

A: What was your brother doing when you got home yesterday?
B: He was eating a sandwich.

d

Jodie, Emma and Luke are shopping in a department store.

Emma: Let's look at the clothes.

Luke: No, thanks! I'm going to the coffee shop.

Emma: **Where's** that?

Luke: Upstairs. See you later.

…

Emma: I like this top!

Jodie: The plain red one?

Emma: No, this striped one. Oh, it's £50. Forget it.

Jodie: **What** do you think of the jeans?

Emma: **Which** ones do you mean?

Jodie: The ones next to the checked jackets.

Emma: Oh yes. **How much** are they?

Jodie: Let's have a look … oh, £125!

Emma: Maybe not then.

[mobile phone rings]

Emma: **Whose** phone is that? Is it yours?

Jodie: Oh, yes … Hello? Hang on, I can't hear …

…

Emma: **Who** was it?

Jodie: Luke. He's bored.

Emma: I've got an idea.

Jodie: **What** is it?

Emma: Let's find a cheaper place!

1 🎧 **Listen and read. Where is Luke phoning from?**

2 **Match the beginnings (1–5) to the endings (a–e) to make true sentences.**

1 – d

1 The striped top is …   a) £125.

2 The jeans are …   b) checked.

3 The jackets are …   c) in an expensive shop.

4 The phone call is …   d) £50.

5 The friends are …   e) from Luke.

Wh- questions

Which ones do you mean?
What do you think of the jeans?
Where's that?
How much are they?
Whose phone is that?
Who was it?
What is it?

Question words
• What • Who • Which • Where • When
• Why • How • What time • What sort/kind of
• Whose
• How much • How many • How long
• How old • How far • How often

3 Complete the questions with the words from the box.

• Whose • Where • How far • How much
• Why • Who (x2) • What • What sort of
• When • How • What time

1 A: _How_ did you get here?
  B: By bus.
2 A: ___ 's your name?
  B: Emma.
3 A: ___ bag is this?
  B: It's mine, thanks.
4 A: ___ was that?
  B: My brother.
5 A: ___ is this, please?
  B: It's £2.20.
6 A: ___ are you running?
  B: Because I'm late.
7 A: ___ do you sit next to?
  B: I sit next to Luke.
8 A: ___ films do you like?
  B: Comedies.
9 A: ___ did you go to bed last night?
  B: Ten o'clock.
10 A: ___ is your party?
  B: It's on Saturday.
11 A: ___ is your school from here?
  B: About a kilometre.
12 A: ___ are you going?
  B: Home.

4a 🎧 05 Listen to parts of six phone calls and respond with questions.

1 Sorry, what's your name?

b 🎧 06 Now listen and check.

Clothes

5a Work in pairs. How many words can you add to the lists in two minutes?

Clothes:
top, dress, …

Styles:
casual, …

Accessories:
scarf, …

Patterns:
flowery, …

b Now check the Word bank on page 56.

6a Look at the photos and answer the questions below.

1 Who's wearing a flowery shirt? *Luke*
2 Whose top is blue and white? *Emma's*
3 Who's in a plain, red top?
4 Who's wearing a belt?
5 Which two are wearing blue jeans?
6 Whose scarf is striped?

b Work in pairs. Take turns to ask similar questions about the people in your class. Use words from Exercise 5a.

A: Whose sweater is green?   *B: Mario's.*

7 Look at the photos on pages 10 and 11. What do you think of the clothes?

1a I'm going to apply.

Grammar Future with *going to* and *will*
Vocabulary Types of music and musical instruments

Star Struck School of Performing Arts

[🏠 Home] [Join in!]

Interested? Come to our <u>Open Day</u>. You won't find a better way to make your dreams come true!

Auditions 1st and 2nd March

FAQs

What will the audition be like?
We'll ask you to perform two pieces. Then there'll be a short interview … and that's it!

What qualifications will I get?
You'll take all the normal school exams (GCSE and A levels) as well as public examinations in Dance, Drama or Music. In addition, you'll leave school with your own portfolio – a record of all your achievements.

Will there be the chance to appear in West End shows?
Maybe! Every year, our students appear in all kinds of shows in and around London.

What musical instruments can I study at the school?
Our students study all kinds of instruments, from voice to double bass! We have an excellent orchestra as well as choirs and bands performing all kinds of music including classical, rock, jazz and pop.

Jess: Hey Toby, have a look at this webpage for <u>StarstruckSchool</u>. It's their Open Day tomorrow.
Toby: Are you going to have a look round?
Jess: Yes, I'm going to apply for an audition.
Toby: Wow! Do you think you'll get in?
Jess: Who knows? But I'm going to try!
Toby: What do your parents say?
Jess: They're cool about it – but hey, it probably won't happen. It sounds like the audition is going to be quite hard. In fact, I think I'll go and practise now.
Toby: Well, don't get a sore throat! Good luck, I'll keep my fingers crossed. ☺

Read

1 🎧 01 Listen and read the webpage and the messages. How is Star Struck School different from yours?

Comprehension

2 Match the beginnings (1–6) to the endings (a–f) to make true sentences.

1 – e

1 Jess wants to study at
2 First of all, she has to do
3 Students at the school take
4 Some students get parts in
5 Students can study
6 They can join bands and

a) an audition.
b) London shows.
c) all kinds of music.
d) choirs.
e) the Star Struck School.
f) public exams.

1 PERFORMANCE

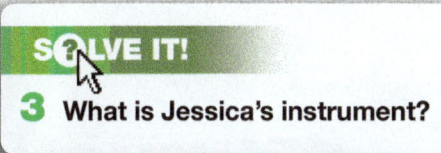

SOLVE IT!

3 What is Jessica's instrument?

Vocabulary: Types of music and musical instruments

4a (02) **Recall** **Listen and name the types of music (1–6). Then check the Word bank on page 56.**

1 pop

b (03) **Extension** **Listen and repeat. Then find these instruments in the picture below. Which one can't you see?**

- cello • clarinet • double bass • drums
- flute • guitar • keyboard • piano
- saxophone • trumpet • violin • voice

Grammar

Future with *going to* and *will*

I'm **going to apply**.
The audition **is going to be** quite hard.
Do you think you**'ll get in**?
It probably **won't happen**.
I think I**'ll go** and practise now.
I**'ll keep** my fingers crossed

Complete the rules.

We use ¹___ for plans and intentions and when we use present evidence to make predictions.
We use ²___ for predictions, promises and decisions.

Practice

5 **Complete the sentences with the correct form of *will* or *going to*.**

1 This music is great. I think I/download/it
   I think I'll download it.
2 This film is really sad. I/cry
3 We should call the police. They/help/us
4 Your exam probably/not be/difficult
5 It's Jo's birthday tomorrow. What/you give/her?
6 I'm busy now. I/do it tomorrow

6 **Complete the conversation with the correct form of *will* or *going to*.**

Toby: Good luck with your audition, Jess. What ¹*are you going to sing* (you/sing) for them?

Jess: I ²___ (sing) some Gershwin. Help, I'm so nervous, I feel terrible!

Toby: Don't worry, you ³___ (be) fine! What ⁴___ (you/wear)?

Jess: I don't know! I think I ⁵___ (probably buy) something new.

Toby: That ⁶___ (be) good. So, what kind of questions ⁷___ (they/ask) you?

Jess: I have no idea. Please stop the questions.

Toby: OK, OK. I ⁸___ (not ask) another thing!

Listen

7 (04) **Listen to Toby and Jess and choose the correct options.**

1 Jess **is waiting for** / knows the result of the audition.
2 She's **happy** / **upset**.
3 She will probably **go out** / **stay at home** later.
4 She **will** / **won't** see Toby often.
5 Toby thinks she **is** / **will be** a star.

Speak and write

8a **Talk about you. Ask and answer the questions in pairs.**

- What types of music do you like?
- Who are your favourite performers?
- Do you ever go to live concerts?
- Do you play any instruments?
- Which instrument(s) would you like to play?

b **Write your answers to the questions in sentences.**

Extra practice

▶ **For more practice, go to page 52.**

1b I'm going out.

Grammar Present continuous for future arrangements

Function Make arrangements: invite, accept, refuse (with excuses)

Dialogue

1  **Listen and read. What are Jodie's plans for next weekend?**

> **Jodie:** Hi, Martin.
> **Martin:** Hi. Can I stand under your umbrella?
> **Jodie:** Yes, sure. Listen, it's my birthday this Saturday, and …
> **Martin:** Oh, *are* you *having* a party?
> **Jodie:** No, I'm *going out* with Luke and some friends. Would you like to come?
> **Martin:** Sure, thanks. I'd love to.
> **Jodie:** Great! We're all *meeting* at our place at six.
> **Martin:** That's fine. … Oh no, hang on, I can't!
> **Jodie:** Why? What's the matter?
> **Martin:** I have to stay at home with Jamie on Saturday. My mom and dad *are visiting* friends.
> **Luke:** Hey guys. What's up?
> **Jodie:** Martin *isn't coming* on Saturday. He can't make it – he's *babysitting*.
> **Luke:** Well, what about going to the cinema on Sunday? *Batman*'s on.
> **Martin:** Cool. I'd love to!
> **Jodie:** Great. I'll have two birthdays!

Comprehension

2 Answer true (T) or false (F).

1 Jodie's birthday is on Saturday. *T*
2 Martin wants to go out with them.
3 He's going to change his plans for Saturday.
4 He has to go out with his parents.
5 Jodie decides to change Saturday's arrangements.
6 They decide to go to the cinema.

Phrases
- hang on
- What's up?
- (He) can/can't make it.

Grammar

Present continuous for future arrangements

Are you **having** a party?
I'm going out with Luke.
Martin **isn't coming** on Saturday.

Note

We often use a time phrase, like *this weekend*, *on Saturday*, *in May*, *at 2 p.m.* with the present continuous for future arrangements.

Choose the correct option.

We use the present continuous for a fixed future plan / prediction.

Practice

3 Look at Luke and Jodie's family calendar. Write sentences about their arrangements.

Mon	Dad - start new job!
Tues	Luke - dentist's 4.00 go to football practice 4.15 Jodie - meet Ann after school
Wed	Mum and Dad - visit Grandma
Thurs	Luke - dentist's 4.30 Jodie - study for English exam
Fri	Jodie - hairdresser's 5.00
Sat	Jodie - hairdresser's 11.00 Evening: Luke and Jodie - have pizza with friends
Sun	Luke and Jodie - cinema

1 *On Monday, their dad's starting a new job.*
2 *On Tuesday, Luke isn't going to the …*

Speak

4 Think of two arrangements for next weekend, one true and one false. Ask and answer about your arrangements. Guess the true arrangement.

A: What are you doing next weekend?
B: I'm going shopping and I'm also playing basketball.
A: You aren't playing basketball, you're going shopping.

Pronunciation: /eɪ/ gr**ea**t, /aɪ/ l**i**ke

5 🎧 1 06 Go to page 58.

Use your English: Make arrangements: invite, accept, refuse (with excuses)

6 🎧 1 07 Listen and repeat. Then practise the conversation in pairs.

A: Would you like to go to a music festival?
B: That sounds good. When is it?
A: It's on Saturday 4th August. Is that OK?
B: Yes, fine. Where is it?
A: It's in Finsbury Park. Do you fancy going?
B: Yes, that would be great. Thanks.

Invite
Would you like to go to a music festival?
Do you want to go to the cinema?
Do you fancy going skateboarding?
What about going into town?

Accept
Yes, that sounds fun/great.
Thanks, that would be great.
Sure. I'd love to.

Refuse (with excuses)
I'm afraid I can't. I'm busy.
Sorry, I can't. I'm babysitting.
I'd like to, but my grandparents are visiting.
I don't really fancy it, but thanks.
Thanks for asking, but I don't think I can.

7a Practise similar conversations about the events below.

What?	When?	Where?
an 80s disco!	on Sat 5th Oct	at the Youth Club
a fireworks display	on Sat 2nd Nov	in City Park
a fashion show	on Fri 8th Nov	in the Town Hall

b Now invite your partner to other events.

Extra practice

▶ For more practice, go to page 52.

1c They're the best films ever!

Grammar Comparison of adjectives: *much* + comparative adjective *(not) as … as*
Superlatives

Vocabulary Adjectives of opinion

Reviews

DVD > film > box sets > reviews

***What's your favourite box set?
Here's your chance to tell us
what you think. Read other
people's opinions and rate
them, too.***

I think the *Lord of the Rings* and *The Hobbit* are the best films ever! The three *LOTR* films are scarier and more exciting than *The Hobbit*, but *The Hobbit* films are less complicated. The plot gets much more confusing in *LOTR*! The actors in *The Hobbit* are as brilliant as the actors in *LOTR*. My absolute favourite is Andy Serkis (Gollum). **GANDALFTHEGREY** *55 minutes ago*

⬆ 10 ⬇ 6

I'm a big *X-Men* fan, but the later ones are a bit disappointing – they aren't as good as the first three. I think the *Spider-Man* films are much better. I didn't like the third one much (it was a bit dull), but the last one is amazing.
FILMFREAK3 *3 hours 35 minutes ago*

⬆ 12 ⬇ 0

The *X-Men* series are my favourite films, without a doubt. They're all fantastic, but in my opinion *X-Men First Class* is the most enjoyable of all. It has great action scenes and the special effects look amazing. The acting is excellent and the music is awesome. **XMENROCK** *4 hours ago*

⬆ 6 ⬇ 2

Personally I don't like films about superheroes. I prefer funny ones, like *Men in Black*. The first two films are much older than the third, but they're still pretty good and very amusing. The third one is much funnier than the others, but it's also more violent. Don't watch it with your little brother or sister. **OXFORDBOY** *4 hours 10 minutes ago*

⬆ 7 ⬇ 0

Get started

1 What was the last film you saw?
What was it like?

Read

2 🔊 Listen and read the online film
reviews. Who makes only positive
comments?

Comprehension

3 **What is the name of the film series and who is speaking?**

1 'I really like them all except one.' *Spider-Man – filmfreak3*
2 'All the films are very good, but one of them is extra special.'
3 'They're great – but difficult!'
4 'They're good, but some of them aren't great.'
5 'They all make me laugh.'

Vocabulary: Adjectives of opinion

4a 🎧 **1 09 Listen and repeat. Which words are usually positive and which are usually negative?**

Positive: *amazing, ...*
Negative: *awful, ...*

> • amazing • awesome • awful • boring
> • brilliant • complicated • confusing
> • disappointing • dull • enjoyable • exciting
> • frightening • funny • interesting • sad
> • scary • violent

b **Which words have the same meaning? Which ones are opposites?**

c **Match words in Exercise 4a to the sentences.**

1 I enjoyed it. It was *enjoyable*.
2 Hmmm, I didn't really understand it.
  It was ___ / ___.
3 There were lots of fights. It was ___.
4 I hid behind the sofa! It was ___ / ___ .
5 I really wanted to see it but then I didn't like it.
  It was ___.
6 It made me laugh. It was ___.
7 I cried! It was ___.
8 The film was very, very good.
  It was ___ / ___ / ___.
9 Sorry, I fell asleep halfway through!
  It wasn't ___ / ___ – it was ___ / ___.
10 I hated it. It was very bad. It was ___.

Grammar

Comparison of adjectives
much + comparative adjective
I think the *Spider-Man* films are **much better/ worse**. The third one is **much funnier** than the others. They're **much more/less exciting**.
(not) as ... as
They are(**n't**) **as good as** the first three.
Superlatives
X-Men First Class is **the most/least enjoyable** of all. They're **the best/worst** films ever!

Practice

5 **Write sentences to compare the three films. Use superlatives, *(not) as ... as* or *(much)* and comparative adjectives. Then compare sentences with your partner.**

FILM	scary	exciting	good
The Midnight Man	***	*	***
No Time Like Now	****	*****	*****
Come Back Soon	*	**	*

1 *The Midnight Man* (scary)
  'The Midnight Man' isn't as scary as 'No Time Like Now' but it's much scarier than 'Come Back Soon'.
2 *Come Back Soon* (exciting)
3 *No Time Like Now* (good)
4 *Come Back Soon* (bad)
5 *No Time Like Now* (scary)
6 *The Midnight Man* (exciting)

Speak

6 **Work in pairs. Choose three film series that you like. Give each one a score from one to five stars for the adjectives in the box. Then discuss your ideas with the class.**

> • exciting • funny • good • interesting
> • sad • scary

We think the Matrix films are better than X-Men, but they aren't as good as Spider-Man. The first Spider-Man film is ...

Write

7 **Read the reviews in Exercise 2 again. Then write about the three film series you chose in Exercise 6, using adjectives of opinion.**

... are great films, but in my opinion they aren't as good as ... I think ...

Extra practice

▶ **For more practice, go to page 52.**

1d Music festivals

Music festivals around the world

SKILLS FOCUS: READING

ACROSS CULTURES

Get started

1 Look at the photos. What's the most famous music festival in your country?

Read

> **READING TIP: HOW TO PREPARE FOR READING**
>
> When you prepare for reading, look at the title, pictures and the headings. This will help you to understand the text.
> Now do Exercise 2.

2a Read the text quickly, then match the photos (A–D) to the paragraphs (1–4).

b 🎧 Read the text again and match the headings (a–d) to the paragraphs (1–4). Then listen and check.

a) Rock band wants prize
b) All kinds of African music
c) A wide range of music and nationalities
d) Music and youth around the world

Comprehension

3 Read the text. Choose the correct options.

1 The text is ___.
  a) an interview   b) a magazine article
  c) an encyclopedia entry
2 The International Festival in Wales is a ___ festival.
  a) jazz   b) rock   c) music and dance
3 Emma thinks it will be ___ to get to the semi-finals.
  a) difficult   b) easy   c) impossible
4 Sanjay is going to ___ the Mumbai Rock Festival.
  a) watch   b) compete at   c) rehearse at
5 The music festival in Zanzibar takes place ___.
  a) in the old city centre   b) in a field
  c) in a football stadium
6 Farrokh is going to ___ at the music festival in Zanzibar City.
  a) perform   b) work   c) compete

1 ___

All around the world young people are going to festivals to listen to music, to perform and to take part in competitions. We meet three teenagers from different countries and ask about their experiences.

2 ___

Emma tells us about The Llangollen International Music Festival that takes place every July in a small town in Wales. 'Each year people come from many different countries. There's lots of choral music, folk singing and dancing as well as classical music. The concerts and competitions take place inside an enormous marquee. My school choir's going to compete in the youth choir competition. It will be tough but we hope to get to the semi-finals.'

3 ___

Sanjay is the lead singer in rock band Tin Heads. 'People don't usually think we have rock and heavy metal in India, but there are millions of people who are into this type of music,' he says. This year Sanjay's band is competing on day one of the Independence Rock Festival in Mumbai. I-Rock is the oldest and the biggest rock festival in India. 'If you win, you get a cash prize and expensive music gear. We rehearse a lot and we want to win.'

A

B

C

4

Farrokh lives in Zanzibar City, which has one of the most important music festivals on the African continent. The festival takes place in an old fort in the historical centre of the city, called Stone Town. 'It's an amazing African party', Farrokh tells us. 'You can hear all types of music here: traditional, fusion, reggae, jazz and hip-hop. The musicians come from all over Africa. During the festival I help backstage with food and drinks so I get to meet many of the famous bands!'

D

NEW WORDS

- perform • take place • choral
- marquee • choir • compete • tough
- semi-finals (of a competition)
- be into (something) • cash • gear
- rehearse • fort • fusion • backstage

Speak

4 **Work in pairs. Answer the questions.**

1 Which of the festivals in the photos would you like to go to? Why?/Why not?
2 Do you know any music festivals or competitions in other countries?
3 Can you play a musical instrument?

Listen

5 🎧 1.11 **Listen to two conversations. Choose the correct options.**

1 There are more than 150 / 50 music festivals in the UK every year.
2 Len mentions rock, jazz and **dance / hip-hop** festivals.
3 Len thinks the 'Big Chill' music festival is much **bigger / better** than Glastonbury.
4 Robert is playing in **a rock band / an orchestra** this weekend.
5 Robert thinks performing at the Royal Albert Hall is **a bit scary / exciting**.

Project

6 **Imagine you are going to organise a youth music festival in your home town. Write a paragraph for the school website about your plans.**

- Where is it going to be?
- What type of competitions/awards are there going to be? (Best Singer, Best Rock Band, etc.)
- What are the prizes going to be?
- Are you going to invite any famous musicians?

We are going to organise …

SKILLS FOCUS: WRITING AN INFORMAL EMAIL

Get ready to write

1 **Read the email. Who is it from and what is it about?**

To: joanne_98@emailme.com

Subject: Saturday night!

1 ¹Hi Jo,

2 ²How are you? I hope you're having a good break after your exams.

3 Do you like The Indigoes? A group of my school friends are going to see them on Saturday. Do you fancy coming with us? Danny's got flu so he wants to sell his ticket (it's £10).

4 The concert starts at eight in the town hall. We're meeting at 6.30 and we're going to have a pizza first. I think it finishes at about half past ten. My dad can give us a lift home.

5 It's going to be a really good evening – I hope you can make it!

³Speak soon,

Sam

2 **Complete the missing words.**

The **Indigoes**

Live concert
at the ¹___ on
² ___ 3rd November
at ³ ___ p.m.

Tickets cost ⁴___.

3 **Read the email again and match the sections in the email (1–5) to the correct headings (A–E).**

1 – B

A Details and arrangements
B Greeting
C Summary and conclusion
D Main message
E Introduction

WRITING TIP: INFORMAL EMAILS
You can start an informal email with *Dear (John),* ... but you can also start it with *Hi!* or *Hello!* End it with a friendly expression, for example: *See you soon, Bye for now, Speak soon, Love* or even just a *x* after your name.
Now do Exercise 4.

4 **Look at the email in Exercise 1. Replace the words and phrases in red (1–3) with a word and phrase from the box (there are two choices for each). Then compare with a partner.**

- Bye for now • Dear • Hello
- How are things with you?
- How's it going? • Love

1 Dear Jo ...

Write

5 **Look at the information below. Write an email to a friend. Invite him/her to join you and Carl on Friday evening. Use the headings in Exercise 3 as a guide.**

C U @ Benji's café @ 6 – Let's have a snack before it starts!
Carl

TALENT SHOW

On Friday 14th March at Seldon High School.
7.30–9.30
Adults £5
Students £3

Language Revision

Grammar (15 marks)

1 Choose the correct options.

0 We'll go / ('re going) to the cinema tomorrow. Do you want to come?
1 In the future robots **will / are going to** play musical instruments.
2 They're planning their holidays. They**'re going to go / 'll go** to Italy.
3 Are you coming out with us tomorrow night? Sorry, **I'll go / 'm going** to a concert.
4 I really like that music. I think I**'m going to / 'll** download it right now.
5 We can't come to the party. We**'ll stay / 're staying** with my uncle this weekend.
6 I feel nervous. I think I**'ll practise / 'm practising** my audition song again.
7 It probably **won't rain / isn't raining** today.

.../7

2 Complete the sentences so they mean the same.

0 *Batman* is more exciting than *Spider-Man*.
Spider-Man isn't as exciting as *Batman*.
1 The first film wasn't as good as the second one.
The second film was ___ the first one.
2 Jessica is more intelligent than Emma.
Emma ___ as Jessica.
3 This film is better than all the others.
This is ___ film.
4 *Toy Story 2* isn't as funny as *Toy Story 3*.
Toy Story 3 is ___ *Toy Story 2*.

.../8

Vocabulary (16 marks)

3 Write the musical instrument.

0 efutl *flute*
1 oenphxoas ___
2 arnietcl ___
3 noiap ___
4 turiga ___
5 elolc ___
6 oybkedar ___
7 sumdr ___
8 utemptr ___

.../8

4 Complete the adjectives.

0 I fell asleep because the film was very b*oring*.
1 I didn't understand the story. It was c___d and c___g.
2 I was really frightened. It was a very s___ film.
3 The photography was aw__e, but the plot was d___g and d___l.
4 Well done! Your project on the Romans was ex___ and very f___y!

.../8

Phrases/Use your English (9 marks)

5 Complete with phrases from the box.

• hang on! • What's up? • can't make it!

A: Hi, Sarah. ¹___
B: I'm organising my party. Are you coming?
A: When is it?
B: Next Friday.
A: Oh no! I ²___ I'm going to Adel's party.
B: That's a shame!
A: Oh, ³___ I can come after all. Adel's party is on Saturday.

.../3

6 Look at the jumbled conversation. Number the lines in the correct order.

☐ a) What about going on Sunday afternoon?
☐ b) Great! What time does the film finish?
☑ c) Would you like to see the new *Batman* film with me on Saturday afternoon?
☐ d) I'd like to, but I'm babysitting my brother in the evening.
☐ e) Good idea! I love pizza.
☐ f) Yes, Sunday's better. Do you fancy going for a pizza after the film?
☐ g) It finishes at 7 p.m., a perfect time to go for a meal!

.../6

LISTEN AND CHECK YOUR SCORE

Grammar	.../15
Vocabulary	.../16
Phrases/Use your English	.../9
Total	**.../40**

2a I've just told you.

Grammar Present perfect simple with time adverbials *ever, never, already, just, yet*

Vocabulary Household jobs

Phrases
- How do you know?
- good for you!
- ha ha, very funny
- you do that

Dialogue

1 🎧 2/01 Listen and read. Why does Jodie need her calculator?

Luke:	Have you been in my room, Jodie?
Jodie:	Yes, I was looking for my calculator.
Luke:	I've already looked. It isn't in there.
Jodie:	How do you know? Your room's a mess. Have you ever made your bed?
Luke:	Of course I have. Anyway, yours isn't much better. I've never seen it tidy.
Jodie:	Actually, I'm sorting it out right now.
Luke:	Well, good for you! Have you found the carpet yet?
Jodie:	Oh, ha ha, very funny. I'm going to take some old clothes to a charity shop in a minute.
Luke:	OK, you do that and I'll finish my Maths homework. I bet you haven't started yours yet.
Jodie:	True, I haven't. But that's because I can't.
Luke:	Why? What do you mean?
Jodie:	I've just told you. I can't find my calculator.

Comprehension

2 Answer true (T), false (F) or doesn't say (DS).

1 Jodie can't find her calculator. T
2 Luke had it yesterday.
3 Jodie's room is always tidy.
4 They've both got Maths homework.
5 Luke has got the calculator.

Vocabulary: Household jobs

3 🎧 **Recall** **Complete the phrases with the words from the box. Then check the Word bank on page 56. Listen and repeat.**

> • do (x 7) • empty • lay • make (x 2) • take
> • tidy • wash

1 *make* breakfast
2 ___ the bed
3 ___ the car
4 ___ the cleaning
5 ___ the ironing
6 ___ the rubbish out
7 ___ the table
8 ___ the vacuuming
9 ___ the washing
10 ___ the washing-up
11 ___ your room
12 ___ the cooking
13 ___ the shopping
14 ___ the dishwasher

Grammar

Present perfect simple with time adverbials *ever, never, already, just, yet*

I've **already** **looked**.
Have you **ever made** your bed?
I've **never seen** it tidy.
I've **just told** you.
Have you **found** the carpet **yet**?
You **haven't started** yours **yet**.

> **Note**
>
> The verb *go* has two past participles, *gone* and *been*.
> *He's gone to his room.* (He's in it now.)
> *He's been in his room.* (He was there but isn't there now.)

Complete the rules.

The words ¹___, ²___, ³___ and ⁴___ usually come between the auxiliary and the main verb.
The word ⁵___ usually comes at the end of a sentence.

Practice

4 **Recall** **Write the past participle form of the verbs. Then check the irregular verb list on page 61.**

be – been   buy – bought

> • be • buy • come • do • eat • find • get
> • go • have • hear • lose • make • meet
> • put • read • run • say • see • sing • sit
> • spend • take • think

5 **Write sentences with the present perfect form of the verbs and *just, yet, already* or *never*.**

1 she/see/the film
She's already seen the film.

4 he/see/a tiger before

2 I/not make/the bed

5 the train/not arrive

3 you/finish/that book?

6 he/have/a bath

6 **Put the word in brackets in the correct place in the sentence. Then ask and answer in pairs.**

1 Have you ⌄cooked a meal? (ever)
  ever
  Have you ever cooked a meal?
  Yes, I have./No, I haven't.
2 Have you had your sixteenth birthday? (yet)
3 Have you broken a bone? (ever)
4 Have you had lunch? (just)
5 Have you performed in a concert? (ever)
6 Have you learnt to drive? (yet)

Write and speak

7a **Work in pairs. Write three more *Have you ever ... ?* questions.**

b **Find a new partner. Take turns to ask and answer the new questions.**

Extra practice

➤ For more practice, go to page 53.

2b He asked me out.

Grammar	Present perfect simple and past simple Time adverbials
Vocabulary	Relationship words and phrases
Function	Talk about problems: suggestions and advice

Read

1 🎧 2.03 Listen and read the problem page. Who's got the worst problem? Why do you think so?

PROBLEMS?
TAMSIN IS HERE TO HELP.

HOME   **ADVICE**

> My girlfriend often borrows money from me, but she doesn't always give it back. Yesterday she borrowed £10 because she wanted to buy me a present – crazy! I don't want to break up with her, but I've lent her quite a lot over the past few months and I'm getting a bit annoyed. Help!
>
> *Mike, 16*

> I go around in a group of three. Most of the time we get on well, but a few weeks ago the other two had a big argument. They haven't made up yet – it's going on and on and I hate it. I don't know what to do, it's driving me mad.
>
> *Jules, 15*

> I'm worried about my best friend. He's missed a lot of school recently, in fact last week he stayed away for three days. I don't think his parents know. I haven't told my mum and dad because I don't want to get him into trouble. What should I do?
>
> *Luke, 16*

> Up to now, the boy next door has been one of my best friends. We've always been like brother and sister. Then last weekend he asked me out. I was really shocked. I don't think of him like that. I said 'No' and now he doesn't speak to me. I feel terrible.
>
> *Josie, 15*

Comprehension

2 Answer the questions in pairs. Who ...

1 bought Mike a present? *his girlfriend*
2 paid for it?
3 has two best friends?
4 doesn't go to school every day?
5 surprised a friend?
6 has upset a friend?

Vocabulary: Relationship words and phrases

3 🎧 2.04 Listen and repeat. Which ones are positive and which are negative?

Positive: *ask somebody out, ...*
Negative: *argue (with), ...*

- argue/have an argument (with)
- ask somebody out • be/get annoyed (with)
- be friends (with) • break up (with)
- fall in love (with) • fall out (with)
- get divorced (from) • get engaged/married (to)
- get on well (with) • go out (with) • make up

Grammar

Present perfect simple and past simple

Name the tenses.

1 She **wanted** to buy me a present.
2 I**'ve lent** her quite a lot.
3 He **stayed** away for three days.
4 I **haven't told** my mum and dad.

Complete the rules.

We use the ¹___ tense to refer to finished time.
We use the ²___ tense when the past still affects
  the present.

Practice

4 **Make five true sentences using the time
  adverbials in the box.**

I started school eight years ago.
I've just had lunch.

- ago • already • at one o'clock • ever
- in 2013 • just • last night • never
- on Saturday • recently • so far • yet
- this morning • up to now • yesterday

5 **Write sentences. Use the present perfect or
  the past simple.**

1 when/they/start/going out?
  When did they start going out?
2 you/ever/fall in love?
3 they/not/make up/yet
4 he/phone/her/yet?
5 when/they/break up?
6 she/never/argue/with him
7 they/meet/last year
8 my parents/get married twenty years ago

Speak

6 **Ask and answer about the things in the box.**

A: Have you ever been to a wedding?
B: Yes, I have. I went to one last year.
A: Whose wedding did you go to?
B: I went to my cousin's wedding. It was fun.

- go to a wedding • lose something important
- have flu • be on a plane • see an elephant
- meet a famous person

Use your English: Talk about problems: suggestions and advice

7 **Listen and repeat. Then practise the
  conversation in pairs.**

A: You look fed up. What's the matter?
B: I'm a bit worried about my homework.
A: Why? Is it difficult?
B: No, not really. But I haven't got time to
  do it.
A: Well, why don't you talk to your teacher?
  Perhaps you can do it tomorrow.
B: Yes, good idea. Thanks.

Ask about a problem
You look a bit miserable/worried/fed up.
What's the matter/What's up?

Respond
I'm a bit worried about my homework.
I don't know what to do about my homework.

Suggest and advise
I see. Well, why don't we study together?
Maybe you should stay in and revise this
  weekend.
I don't think you should worry too much.

8 **Work in pairs. Look again at the problems
  in Exercise 1. Then roleplay conversations
  with Mike, Jules, Luke and Josie. Use the
  ideas in the box or your own ideas.**

*A: Hi, Mike, you look fed up. What's the
  matter?*
B: I don't know what to do about ...

- explain how you feel • say 'No!'
- forget your wallet • talk to him/her/them
- discuss it with an adult • relax
- forget about it

Write

9 **Choose one of the conversations from
  Exercise 8. Write the conversation. Use
  Exercise 7 to help you.**

Extra practice

For more practice, go to page 53.

2c People who you can trust.

Grammar Defining relative clauses with *who, which, that, whose, where*
Vocabulary Family

Get started

1 Which would you prefer – to have lots of brothers and sisters, or to be an only child? Why?

Read

2 Listen and read the article. Do you think this article is true about you and your family?

Comprehension

3 Work in pairs. Answer the questions according to the article.

1 When do oldest children become anxious?
When the second child arrives.
2 What negative feelings do youngest children sometimes have?
3 Why do middle children often have lots of friends?
4 What do only children need to learn?
5 How can the only child in a family become the youngest?

KNOW YOUR PLACE!

Are you an only child? Or perhaps you are the oldest, the youngest, or a middle child. Does it matter? Well, yes, it does! The place **where** you are in your family affects your personality.

Oldest children are confident people and natural leaders – but they are sometimes anxious, too. Why? The first child gets lots of attention from parents, grandparents, aunts and uncles. Then the second child arrives. It's a major event **that** changes everything.

Youngest children are usually easy-going people **who** love parties and fun. They often have more freedom than their brothers and sisters. On the other hand, they sometimes think their parents don't care about them. They feel unimportant: they often get clothes and toys **which** the others have used before them.

Middle children make friends easily. They dislike arguments and are good peacemakers (they have to be!). They are people **who** you can trust. However, children **that** are in the middle often feel less special than their brothers and sisters. Things don't always seem fair.

Only children spend a lot of time alone or with adults. This means they are often confident, independent and successful at school. They never have to share their things – that's a lesson they have to learn.

Of course, things change. For example, when the oldest child moves out, the middle child 'moves up'. Perhaps she'll finally get the bedroom **that** she's always wanted! Or think about an only child **whose** parents get divorced. Perhaps he will have stepbrothers and stepsisters one day – then he will suddenly become the oldest, the youngest or a middle child.

Oldest, youngest, middle or only child, it's part of the reason you're you!

Vocabulary: Family

4a **Recall** Name as many family words as you remember. Then check the Word bank on page 56.

b (2/07) **Extension** Listen and repeat. Then complete the sentences with the words from the box.

> • daughter/son-in-law • fiancée/fiancé
> • married • mother/father-in-law • single
> • sister/brother-in-law • stepmother/father
> • stepsister/brother

1 My brother's wife is my _sister-in-law_ and she's my parents' ___.
2 My mum got married again. Her second husband is my ___ and his daughter is my ___.
3 My sister is going to marry her ___ next year. Then she won't be ___ anymore.

Grammar

Defining relative clauses: *who, which, that, whose, where*
who/that
Youngest children are usually easy-going people **who/that** love parties. (subject)
They are people (**who/that**) you can trust. (object)
which/that
It's a major event **which/that** changes everything. (subject)
Perhaps she'll finally get the bedroom (**which/that**) she's always wanted! (object)
whose
Think about an only child **whose** parents get divorced.
where
The place **where** you are in your family affects your personality.

Complete the rules.
We use ^{1}___ or ^{2}___ for people and ^{3}___ or ^{4}___ for things.
We use ^{5}___ for places and ^{6}___ for possession.
We can omit ^{7}___, ^{8}___ or ^{9}___ when they refer to the object of the sentence.

Practice

5 Join the sentences. Use *who, which, where* or *whose*. Then, when possible, write a second sentence omitting the relative pronoun.

1 They're the people. I met them last night.
   They're the people who I met last night.
   They're the people I met last night.
2 That's the house. I was born there.
3 They're the toys. I gave them to my sister.
4 She's the girl. She's got four brothers.
5 He's the boy. His brother's just got married.
6 It's a problem. It causes arguments.
7 There's the girl. We were talking about her.
8 This is the book. I need it.

6 Make true sentences. Then compare with a partner.

1 I don't like people who ...
2 I like going on holiday to places where ...
3 I've got some friends who ...
4 I like films which ...
5 I prefer food which ...

Pronunciation: /æ/ family, /ɑː/ father

7 (2/08) Go to page 58.

Listen

8 (2/09) Listen to the conversation and answer true (T) or false (F).

1 Harry is the youngest child in his family. *T*
2 He's got a sister who is married.
3 His niece was born two years ago.
4 His niece's name is Alice.
5 He's got three sisters.
6 Harry's sister Jackie is married to Andy.

> **SOLVE IT!**
>
> **9** Listen again. How old is Alice's mum?

Extra practice

➡ For more practice, go to page 53.

2d The Rock Roses

REAL LIFE ISSUE

'Hey, Ian, what are you doing next Saturday?'

'I don't know. Why?'

'I've got a spare ticket for The Rock Roses concert. My cousin's just dropped out. Do you want to come?'

'You bet I do. Fantastic. Oh, but how much is it?'

'That's just it, it's free. My dad works at the theatre, so he's got a couple of free tickets. How good is that?'

'It's excellent. I can't wait. Thanks, James.'

'No problem. It'll be a blast. See you tomorrow at school.'

Ian put his phone down and went to find his mother.

'Guess what, Mum, James has got me a free ticket for The Rock Roses. Isn't that amazing!'

'That sounds wonderful. Hang on, when is it?'

'This Saturday evening. Why? What's the matter?'

'Ian, that's the day of Danny's birthday party. Don't tell me you've already forgotten?'

Danny was Ian's next-door neighbour. He was three years younger than Ian and he hero-worshipped the older boy. He often called round to visit and he even copied Ian's taste in music and TV programmes. Ian found him quite annoying. It didn't usually matter too much, but this time it mattered a lot.

'Oh no! I don't believe it. I can't miss The Rock Roses! I can see Danny any time!'

'Don't be mean. He's really looking forward to Saturday and I don't think he's invited many people. And you *have* already accepted the invitation, you know.'

'I know, but they're my favourite band. I've always wanted to see them. Are you saying I can't go?'

'Well, Ian, I suppose it's up to you.'

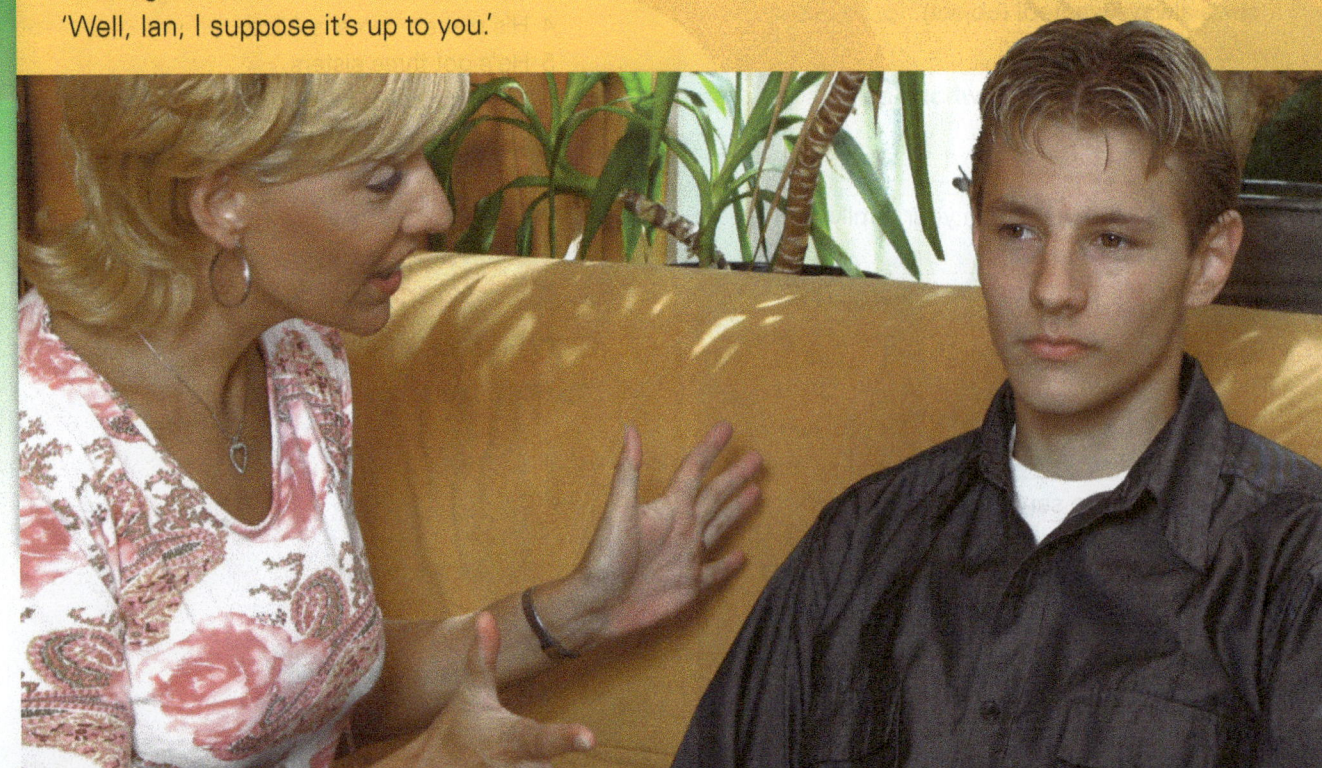

NEW WORDS
- Hey • spare • drop out • That's just it.
- a couple of • blast • guess what
- hero-worship • taste (in music, etc.)
- mean (= unkind)
- look forward to • it's up to (you)

Get started

1 Imagine you can have a free ticket to a concert. Who would you most like to see?

Read

2 **Read the story about Ian. Why is he upset?**

Comprehension

3 Choose the correct options.

1 The spare ticket was James's dad's / cousin's.
2 At first, Ian's mother was **pleased / worried** about the concert.
3 Ian is **the same age as / older than** Danny.
4 Danny is planning a **big / small** party.
5 Ian's mother says he must **go to the party / decide.**

Speak your mind!

> **SPEAKING TIP: SPEAK AS MUCH AS POSSIBLE**
> Get as much practice as possible. Always try to join in conversations and discussions in English. Make sure you always say something.
> Now do Exercise 4.

4a **Work in pairs (AA and BB).**

Students A: Think of three reasons why Ian should go to the concert, not the party. Make notes.

Students B: Think of three reasons why Ian should go to the party, not the concert. Make notes.

b **Make new pairs (AB). Use your notes to roleplay a discussion about what Ian should do.**

A: He should go to the concert because …
B: No, I don't agree. I think …

Write

5 Read Ian's message and write your reply. Give reasons for your advice.

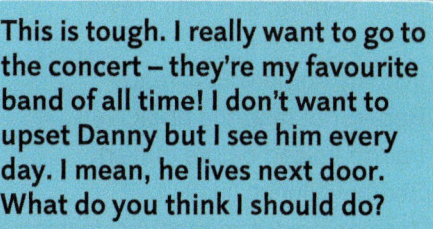

> This is tough. I really want to go to the concert – they're my favourite band of all time! I don't want to upset Danny but I see him every day. I mean, he lives next door. What do you think I should do?

> *Hi Ian.*
> *I can see your problem.*
> *I think …*

Listen

> **LISTENING TIP: LISTEN FOR GIST**
> Listen to the whole recording first, to get a general idea of the meaning. Then listen again for detail. Now do Exercise 6.

6a **Listen to Ian talking to James the next day at school. Choose the correct options.**

1 Ian is going to go to ___.
   a) the party   b) the concert
2 James is ___.
   a) surprised   b) upset
3 James says it's ___.
   a) a problem   b) fine

b **Listen again and answer the questions.**

1 At first, what does James suggest?
2 What two reasons does Ian give for his decision?
3 What does James say about his dad?
4 What does he say about The Rock Roses?

Speak

7 **Do you think Ian was right? Why?/Why not? Tell the class.**

2 Language Revision

Grammar (16 marks)

1 Write sentences. Use the present perfect form of the verbs and the words in brackets.

0 Have/perform/in a play? (ever)
   Have you ever performed in a play?
1 I/do/my homework (already)
2 Robert/not read/the book (yet)
3 I/go/to Ireland before (never)
4 She/have/lunch (just)
5 Jackie's boyfriend/meet/her/parents? (ever)

.../5

2 Complete the conversation with the present perfect or past simple form of the verbs.

A: Hi, Joe. How are you?
B: Fine, thanks. ⁰*I've just come* (just come) back from the USA. ¹___ (you/ever/go) there?
A: Yes, I ²___ (go) two years ago. Where ³___ (you/stay)?
B: We ⁴___ (stay) with some friends in Hollywood.
A: I ⁵___ (never go) to Hollywood! Did you meet anybody famous?
B: No, we didn't. But last week, we ⁶___ (visit) Universal Film Studios.
A: Lucky you!

.../6

3 Choose the correct options.

0 This is the place where / which I was born.
1 She's the girl who / whose brother is on TV.
2 I don't like films who / which are sad.
3 It's my sister Jane whose / who is the actress.
4 They are the people who / whose we met last year.
5 Which sentence doesn't need a relative pronoun? ___

.../5

Vocabulary (14 marks)

4 Complete the phrases (0–4). Then match them to the definitions (a–e).

0 – c

0 *do* the washing
1 ___ the table
2 ___ the washing-up
3 ___ the vacuuming
4 ___ the breakfast

a) wash dirty cups and plates
b) prepare the first meal of the day
c) wash dirty clothes
d) arrange things ready to eat a meal
e) clean the carpet

.../8

5 Complete the sentences.

0 The opposite of 'get married' is 'get *divorced*'.
1 Meg is my mum's mother. My dad is Meg's ___.
2 Before you get married, you get ___.
3 John and Helen are married. They are ___ and wife.
4 If you ___ arguments, you don't ___ on well.
5 If a boy likes a girl, he asks her ___.

.../6

Phrases/Use your English (10 marks)

6 Complete with phrases from the box.

• How do you know? • Good for you.
• Ha ha, very funny. • do that.

A: Have you bought a new phone, Terry?
B: Yes, I have. ¹___
A: Because you're speaking on it all the time!
B: ²___
A: I'm going to buy a new phone, too.
B: ³___
A: I'll phone you every hour.
B: You ⁴___ But I won't always answer!

.../4

7 Match the sentences (0–3) to the sentences (a–d) to make a conversation.

0 – d

0 You look miserable.
1 What's the matter?
2 When did that happen?
3 Maybe you should call him and make up.

a) It was last Friday night. I really regret it.
b) Maybe I should. I miss him!
c) My boyfriend Philip and I have split up.
d) I am.

.../6

🔊 2 12	LISTEN AND CHECK YOUR SCORE	
Grammar		.../16
Vocabulary		.../14
Phrases/Use your English		.../10
Total		**.../40**

Skills Revision

1 _____

2 _____

My mum always asks me to do a lot of things around the house. I do the vacuuming, the washing-up and make the beds. This annoys me because my twin brother Mark doesn't do any jobs. I've told my mum that it's not fair, but she just doesn't listen. Last Tuesday we had a big argument when I refused to take out the rubbish. At the moment we're not speaking to each other and last weekend I stayed with Grandma. She's the only person who listens to me. What should I do?

Trisha 14

3 _____

I'm worried about my best friend, Denise. I think she really likes my boyfriend, Nick. Every time I've met up with him recently, Denise always seems to be there, too. Last Friday I met Nick at a café. Denise was in the café when I arrived! Denise isn't as attractive as me, but she is very funny and Nick laughs at all her jokes! I haven't spoken to her about this yet because I am afraid of falling out with her. I don't know what to do.

Kimberly 15

Read

1 Read the text quickly and match the headings (A–D) to the gaps (1–3). There is one extra heading.

A He's my boyfriend, not yours!
B I've just broken up with him.
C Ask Annie – the problem page for teens
D I'm fed up with household jobs.

2 Read the text again. Answer true (T), false (F) or doesn't say (DS).

0 Trisha does a lot of household jobs. *T*
1 Trisha lives with her grandmother.
2 Trisha isn't speaking to Mark.
3 Denise is going out with Nick.
4 Denise is more attractive than Kimberly.
5 Kimberly doesn't want to have an argument with Denise.

Listen

3a 🎧 2/13 Listen and choose the correct option.

The listening is about ... .
a) shopping   b) a music event   c) a rock concert

b 🎧 2/13 Listen again and choose the correct options.

0 The workshop is about the history of music / musical instruments .
1 At the end of the workshop everybody performs / listens to a concert.
2 Danny has / hasn't been to the event before.
3 At first, Erica thinks it sounds dull / exciting.
4 Erica thinks Tom Sutherland is cool / boring.
5 On Saturday Erica is going shopping / visiting a relative.
6 Erica and Danny are going to the workshop in the morning / afternoon.

Write

4 Write an email to a friend inviting him or her to an event (for example, a concert or a party). Use the headings as a guide.

• greeting
• introduction
• main message
• details and arrangements
• summary and conclusion

Dear Miriam,
How are things with you?

NOW I CAN		
Read	understand letters about problems.	☐
Listen	understand gist and detail in a conversation.	☐
Write	write an invitation.	☐

Grammar   *too* + adjective/adverb + *to*
(not) + adjective/adverb + *enough to*

Vocabulary   Adjectives and nouns of measurement
Transport

Comprehension

2 **Answer the questions in pairs.**

Find ...

1 two ways of crossing the river. *by bridge, ...*
2 an unusual kind of taxi.
3 a slow way to enjoy the sights along the river.
4 two ways to look down on London.
5 a fast but sometimes uncomfortable way to get about.

Read

1 🎧 **Listen and read the webpage. How many types of transport does it mention?**

GETTING AROUND

THE CITY
in style

So, you have a weekend in London. Lucky you! Here's some advice: plan carefully and decide what you want to do. The city's too big to see it all on foot, so what's the best way to get around?

The Tube is quick and easy, but it's often too crowded to find a seat. Some people prefer to catch a bus and of course there's a great view from the top of a double-decker!

If buses aren't stylish enough to tempt you, how about a rickshaw? The rickshaw rider will take you wherever you want to go. Sit back and enjoy the greenest way to travel! Or, if you want to avoid the traffic, go by boat. River buses are popular and they move slowly enough to see the sights along the river.

Back on dry land, you can use one of the many bridges to cross the river – or if you're too tired to walk, use the cable car! The London cable car goes over the Thames at a height of 90 metres. The river there is only one kilometre wide so it's a short trip. At busy times of the day the cable car goes too fast to take good photos. At other times the ride is slower and long enough to enjoy the view.

Grammar

too + adjective/adverb + *to*
The city's **too big to** see it all on foot.
The car goes **too fast to** take photos.

(not) + adjective/adverb + *enough to*
It's (isn't) **long enough to** enjoy the view.
They (don't) move **slowly enough to** see the sights.

Practice

3 Make sentences. Use the prompts and *too ... to* or *(not) ... enough to*.

1 it/be expensive/travel by taxi
It's too expensive to travel by taxi.
2 rickshaws/not be big/carry lots of people
3 I/not dance well/perform in public
4 you/be young/get married
5 David/not study hard/pass his exams
6 Jack/not be strong/carry that box
7 you/be clever/solve the puzzle?
8 Maisie/run slowly/win the race

4 Write sentences about you with *too ... to* or *(not) ... enough to*. Use the ideas in the box or your own ideas.

I'm (not) old enough to have a job.
I'm too young to have a job.

- be old/young – have a job
- run fast/slowly – be in the Olympics
- get up early/late – get to school on time
- sing well/badly – be a pop star
- be fit/unfit – run a kilometre
- be confident/shy – make a speech

Vocabulary: Adjectives and nouns of measurement

5 🎧 3/02 Listen and repeat. Then match the nouns to the adjectives.

age – old

age cost depth distance height length
size speed width

big deep expensive far fast high long
old wide

Listen

6 🎧 3/03 Listen to the talk about the Docklands Light Railway. Complete the notes.

* DLR = [1]<u>Docklands Light Railway</u>
* opened in [2]___
* unusual because [3]___
* started with [4]___ stations and was [5]___ km long
* now [6]___ stations and [7]___ km long
* 200,000 passengers every [8]___
* goes [9]___ ground (mostly)
* speed: [10]___ km per hour

Vocabulary: Transport

7a Look at the types of transport in Exercise 1 again. Write the advantages and disadvantages of each one.

The Tube: quick, easy, often crowded

b Recall How many more types of transport can you name? Check the Word bank on page 57.

car, tram, ...

Speak and write

8 Discuss the questions in pairs or small groups. Then write some travel advice to tourists in your town or city.

- What are the different ways of travelling around your town or city?
- Which ways are the slowest, fastest, cheapest and most expensive?
- Which form of transport do you prefer? Why?

You can travel around our town by tram, ...

Extra practice

➤ For more practice, go to page 53.

3b You can't miss it.

Vocabulary Places in town
Function Ask for and give directions

Vocabulary: Places in town

1 Recall List all the places in town on the map.
Then check the Word bank on page 57.

Martin:	Hey, Emma. Sorry, I'm late. I'm a bit lost.
Emma:	Oh no, where are you? Stupid question! I mean, what can you see?
Martin:	I'm standing in front of Davidson's department store. It's next to a bank.
Emma:	OK, that's Joyner Street. No problem, you aren't too far away. Go right, down Joyner Street to the traffic lights.
Martin:	OK, hang on … right, I've done that!
Emma:	Good. Now go past the cinema. Then take the second turning on the left into West Street.
Martin:	OK, what now?
Emma:	Go straight on until you see a children's playground on your left. You can't miss it. I live opposite the playground … Oh, nice hoodie!
Martin:	How do you know?
Emma:	Look up! Hi there!
Jodie:	Hi, Martin!

Phrases
- I'm a bit lost.
- I mean, …
- what now?

Dialogue

2 🎧 3/04 **Listen and read. Where does Emma live? Find it on the map.**

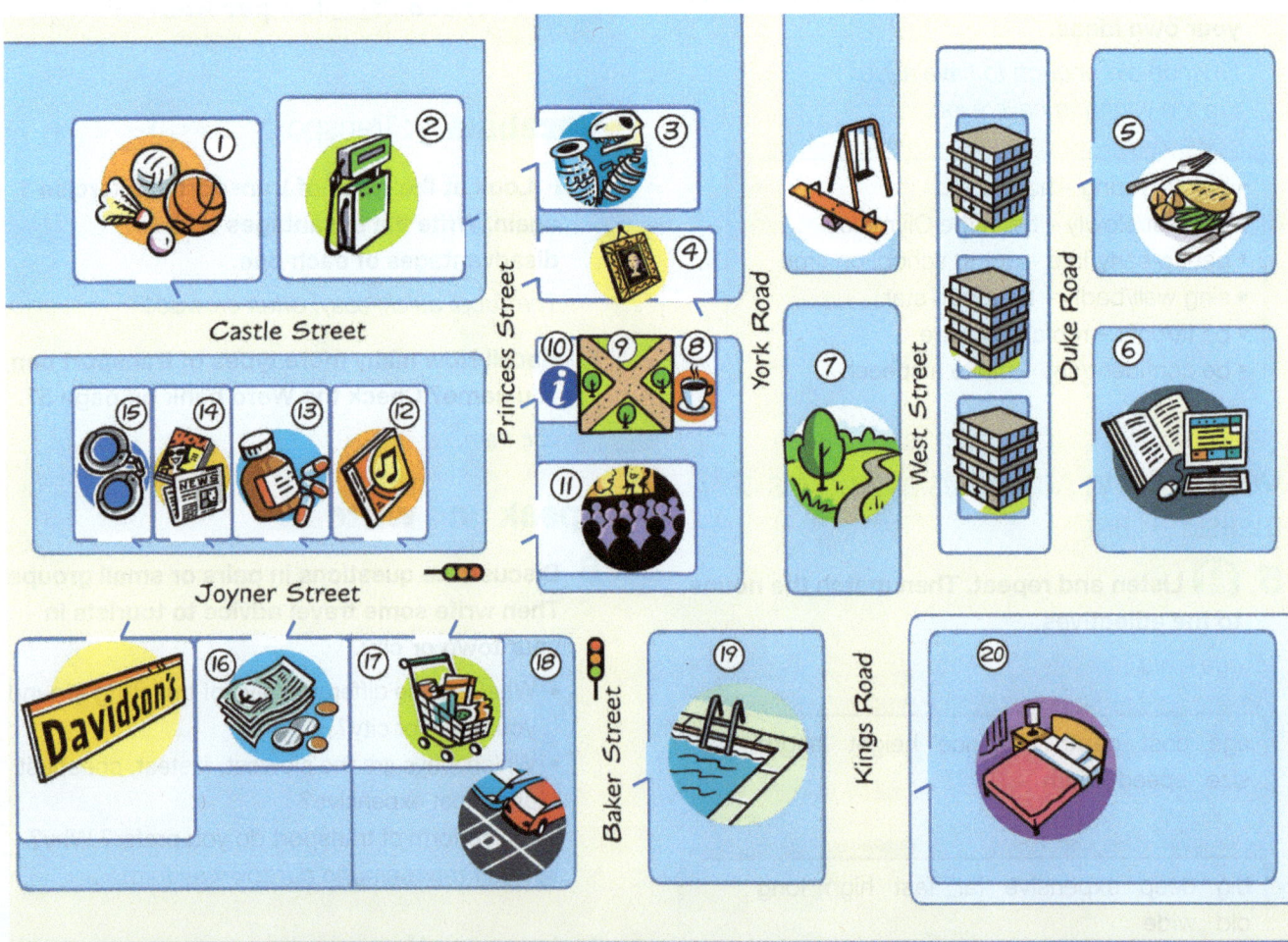

Comprehension

3 **Rewrite the summary, correcting the mistakes.**

Martin is on his way to see Jodie. She phones him because he's late. She gives him directions from the library to her flat. He knows when he gets to the right place because he sees her.

Martin is on his way to see Emma …

Practice

4 **Look at the map on page 34. Then complete the directions with the places in the box. There are three extra places.**

- cinema • park • playground • restaurant
- supermarket

1 Go left out of the sports centre. Cross Princess Street and go straight on, past the square on your right and the art gallery on your left. Turn right and you'll see the ___ on your left.

2 From the bank, cross over the road and turn right. Take the fourth turning on the left. Go past the library and you'll see the ___ on your right.

Listen

5 🎧 ³⁄₀₅ **Look at the map again and listen to two phone conversations. Where are the two people going?**

Pronunciation: Sentence stress and rhythm

6 🎧 ³⁄₀₆ **Go to page 58.**

Use your English: Ask for and give directions

7 🎧 ³⁄₀₇ **Find Davidson's on the map. Listen and repeat. Then practise the conversation in pairs.**

A: Excuse me. Can you tell me the way to the art gallery, please?

B: Yes, sure. Go down Joyner Street until you get to the traffic lights, then turn left. Go straight on, past the tourist information centre. Cross over the road and you'll see it on the right opposite the petrol station. You can't miss it.

A: Thanks very much.

B: No problem. You're welcome.

Ask for directions

Excuse me./Sorry to bother you …

Can you tell me the way to the theatre, please?

How do I get to the theatre?

Where's the nearest theatre, please?

Give directions

Go left out of the library. Turn right at the corner. It's next to the bank.

Take the second/third turning on the left.

See Exercise 4 for other directions.

8 **Work in pairs. Take turns to ask for and give directions to four places on the map.**

Write

9 **Write directions from your home to the nearest shop, station or bus stop.**

Extra practice

➤ **For more practice, go to page 54.**

3c We throw away too many things.

Grammar *too many, too much, not enough*
Pronouns *some-, any-, no-, every-* + *thing, where, one, body*
Vocabulary Countable and uncountable nouns

Read

1 🎧 **Listen and read the webpage. Which is the correct summary?**

a) Do more recycling.   b) Eat less food.   c) Don't throw things away.

**TALKBACK: YOU ASK, WE ANSWER.
TODAY, WE'RE TALKING … RUBBISH!**

Home | News | Articles

> **I know I should recycle things, but why? The refuse collectors collect our rubbish every week. So what's the problem? ben15**

Of course we can't recycle everything, but we throw away far too many things. Each year the average British family throws away about 100 kg of glass, 40 kg of plastic and 260 kg of paper (that's about five trees). That's an awful lot of rubbish! And believe it or not, we throw away about one third of all the food we buy (so we waste a lot of money, too).

Not enough people recycle and too much rubbish goes to landfill sites (enormous holes in the ground). As everything lies there year after year, it poisons the land. It also creates methane (a greenhouse gas that increases global warming). These days, there isn't enough space for all the landfill sites we need – we have to send some of our rubbish overseas!

> **It doesn't matter if I recycle or not. One person can't change anything. nonamegirl**

Not true! Change has to start somewhere – why not with you? And remember this – if nobody does anything, nothing will change!

Comprehension

2 **Answer true (T), false (F) or doesn't say (DS) according to the webpage.**

1 *Ben15* thinks recycling is a waste of time. *DS*
2 The UK uses 260 kg of paper per person every year.
3 British people waste most of the food that they buy.
4 Rubbish in landfill sites pollutes the earth and the air.
5 Some of our rubbish goes to landfill sites in other countries.
6 *nonamegirl* wants to change things.

SOLVE IT!

3 Joe is 16. How much glass (approximately) has his family thrown away in his lifetime?

Vocabulary: Countable and uncountable nouns

4a 🎧 3 09 **Listen and repeat. Put the words from the box in the table.**

- family • food • glass • holes • money • people
- plastic • problem • rubbish • things

Countable	Uncountable
family	*food*

b 🎧 3 10 **Listen and repeat. Now add these words to the table in Exercise 4a.**

- air • children • cities • garden • information
- litter • luggage • music • news • pollution
- school • shop • snow • street • traffic • woman

Grammar

too many, too much, not enough

We throw away far **too many** things.
Too much rubbish goes to landfill sites.
Not enough people recycle.
There **isn't enough** space.

Practice

5 **Choose the correct options in sentences (1–4). Then complete the sentences with the correct form of the verb** *be.*

1 There *'s* too much / many pollution in our towns.
2 There ___ too **much** / **many** rubbish in the streets.
3 There ___ too much / many traffic on the roads.
4 There ___ too **much** / **many** people in the city.
5 There ___ (not) enough parks and playgrounds.
6 ___ there enough food for us?
7 There ___ (not) enough places where we can recycle.
8 There ___ (not) enough clean air.

Grammar

Pronouns *some-, any-, no-, every- + thing, where, one, body*

	some-	*any-*	*no-*	*every-*
thing	something	anything	nothing	everything
place	somewhere	anywhere	nowhere	everywhere
person	somebody	anybody	nobody	everybody
	someone	anyone	no one	everyone

Practice

6 **Complete the sentences with words from the grammar box.**

1 A: What will the Earth be like in a thousand years' time?
  B: *Nobody* knows.
2 A: What shall we do with these old newspapers?
  B: Let's find ___ to recycle them.
3 A: I don't know ___ who grows their own food. Do you?
  B: Yes, my aunt grows vegetables in her garden.
4 A: Let's do ___ about the litter in the playground.
  B: OK, I'll get some rubbish sacks.
5 A: Is there ___ in that bottle?
  B: No, ___. It's empty.
6 A: What a terrible place. There's rubbish ___.
  B: Yes, and there's ___ to sit down.

Listen

7 🎧 3 11 **Listen to Della talking about her town. Read the summaries (1–6) and tick (✓) the ones that are correct.**

1 I live here. ✓
2 There's nothing to do here. ☐
3 My friends and I don't go to the sports club. ☐
4 I like expensive clothes shops. ☐
5 There aren't enough cafés. ☐
6 The streets are dirty. ☐

Speak

8 **Work in pairs or small groups. Talk about your town, and the things you would like to change (traffic, pollution, rubbish, noise, etc.). Then tell the class.**

There's too much traffic. There's nowhere to go in the evenings.

Extra practice

➡ **For more practice, go to page 54.**

3d Sightseeing – by land, sea or air!

SKILLS FOCUS: READING

Get started

1 Look at the photos. Which place looks
a) the most interesting b) the most exciting?

Read

> **READING TIP: HOW TO GUESS THE MEANING OF NEW WORDS**
>
> Use clues to guess the meaning of new words. First, decide what part of speech the word is (e.g. verb, noun or adjective). Then guess what it means from the context (what comes before and after). You can check the meaning in a dictionary later.
> Now do Exercise 2.

2a 🎧 3/12 Read the travel guide quickly. What three cities can you visit? What are the three exciting ways to see them?

b Read the guide again and find these new words. Guess the meaning.

1 junk (line 5)
   'junk' is a noun. I think it is a traditional Chinese boat.
2 beams (line 11)
3 stunning (line 11)
4 villains (line 15)
5 fudge (line 20)
6 barbie (line 33)

Comprehension

3 Answer the questions.

1 What is the best way to see Hong Kong's high buildings?
   From a boat on the harbour.
2 What is the 'Symphony of Lights'?
3 Where can you find ghosts in Edinburgh?
4 What sights can you see in Edinburgh's Royal Mile area?
5 What sights can you see on the helicopter ride?
6 What can you do on Bondi Beach?

TEEN TRAVEL: GUIDE

THREE EXCITING WAYS TO SEE THREE EXCITING CITIES

● HONG KONG, CHINA

Did you know that Hong Kong is actually 260 small islands? This city is famous for its skyline. Hong Kong's skyscrapers are too tall to appreciate from the street, so the best way to see them is from
5 a boat on the harbour. Travel in a traditional junk once used by Chinese fishermen and pirates. You can take a night cruise around Victoria Harbour to see the incredible 'Symphony of Lights'. This is a multimedia light and music show where you can see
10 Hong Kong's highest buildings. They are illuminated with coloured lights and laser beams – it's stunning!

● EDINBURGH, SCOTLAND

If you don't fancy walking, a fun way to see Edinburgh is by rickshaw. You can fit two or three people in this unusual taxi and the driver gives you
15 a guided tour. Learn about the villains and heroes that lived in the old town. Your guide can also tell you tales about the ghosts in Edinburgh's forgotten underground city. If this is too scary, take a break and visit one of Edinburgh's traditional sweet shops –
20 try some home-made fudge, it's delicious! Finish your tour in the area called the Royal Mile, in the old part of the city. At the bottom you can see Holyrood Palace and at the top, Edinburgh Castle.

● SYDNEY, AUSTRALIA

Have you ever been in a helicopter? Take a
25 twenty-minute ride over the city and its beaches. It's amazing to see Sydney's skyscrapers and waterways from the air. The pilot gives a commentary and you can see Sydney Harbour Bridge and Sydney Opera House. The helicopter
30 ride ends at Bondi Beach. This is a popular place for surfers. But if you are not brave enough to go surfing you can relax on the golden beach. And if you're hungry, why not enjoy an Australian 'barbie'? Watch out in January though, because it is summer
35 here and the beach is often too crowded to do anything.

Listen

4 🎧 **Listen to the information about the Sydney 'Hop-on hop-off bus tour'. Complete the notes in the table.**

Bus type:	[1] *Open-air double-decker*
Duration of tour:	[2] ___ minutes
Ticket types:	[3] ___ / ___-hour tickets
Sights:	[4] ___, ___
Language of tour commentary:	[5] ___
Place to start tour:	[6] ___ bus stop
Number of bus stops:	[7] ___

Speak

5 **Work in pairs. Make a list of the places, activities and sights in the guide in Exercise 2. Decide which ones you would recommend for teenagers, older people, or for young children.**

Project

6 **Write a travel blog about a place you went to last summer. Use the ideas below. Include a photo you took, or download one from the internet.**

- Where you went
- Who you went with
- How you got there (means of transport)
- Something exciting that happened
- Your opinion of the place

Last summer I went to London …

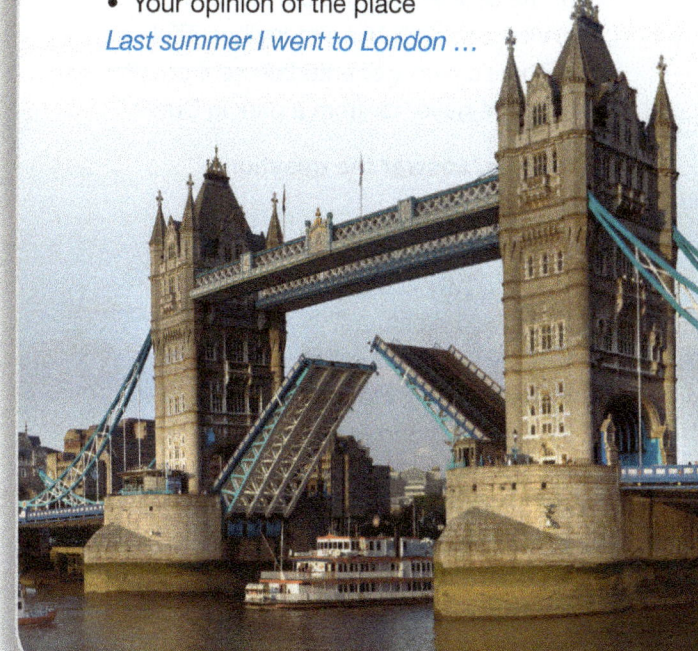

NEW WORDS
- skyline • skyscraper • appreciate
- harbour • pirates • cruise • illuminated
- fit • hero • tales • underground
- home-made • waterways • commentary

3e   A great city

DUBLIN A GREAT CITY

Are you a music-lover, a shopper or do you just want to relax? Dublin offers it all!

¹__ Walk around the historic streets of Temple Bar and explore the wide variety of shops and market stalls. Relax in a riverside café and watch the world go by. This part of the city is a 'must' for tourists – there's something there for everyone!

²__ Check out the many music venues or get tickets for a show or film in one of Dublin's great theatres and cinemas. There are lots of museums and galleries to choose from too, including the very popular Wax Museum Plus, with life-size models of celebrities past and present.

³__ Its shops sell everything from high fashion to paperbacks and pencils. And for something a little bit different, go to the Dublin flea market (you'll need plenty of time!).

⁴__ The most famous one is Phoenix Park – it's one of the biggest city parks in Europe. It's home to many animals and birds, including a magnificent herd of deer. You can see more exotic animals as well, because Dublin Zoo is there, too!

Get ready to write

1 Read the text from a tourist brochure. Complete it with the sentences (a–e). There is one extra sentence.

   1 – b
   a) Shoppers will love the city centre.
   b) The best way to see the city is on foot.
   c) Visit one of Dublin's many beautiful beaches.
   d) There's plenty of entertainment on offer.
   e) You're never far from a park in Dublin.

2 In pairs, answer the questions.
   Where can you:
   1 see models of famous people?
      At the Wax Museum Plus.
   2 see wild creatures?
   3 sit by the river?
   4 buy designer clothes?
   5 see an old part of town?

> **WRITING TIP: PARAGRAPHS AND TOPIC SENTENCES**
> Organise your writing in paragraphs with different topics. You can start each new paragraph with a 'topic sentence' (see a–e above). This tells the reader the main topic of the paragraph.
> Now do Exercise 3.

3 Read the text in Exercise 1 again. Match the paragraphs to the topics in the box. There is one extra topic.

> • Entertainment   • Open spaces   • Shopping
> • Transport   • Walking around the town

Write

4a Work in pairs. You are going to write a text for a tourist brochure about a town or city.
   1 Choose a town or city you both know.
   2 Choose four topics from the box in Exercise 3 and note down your ideas.
   Entertainment: four cinemas, skating rink, theatre
   Shopping: market, …

b Now write the brochure. Think of a title and then write four paragraphs. Start each paragraph with a topic sentence.

   Oxford: my city
   If you're looking for entertainment, Oxford is the place to go. There are four cinemas and they show a wide range of films. There's also …
   You can buy almost anything in Oxford! There's a …

Language Revision

Grammar (14 marks)

1 Complete the sentences. Use *too ... to* or *(not) ... enough to* and the words in brackets.

0 Billy didn't catch the bus. (run fast)
Billy *didn't run fast enough to* catch the bus.

1 They can't get married. (be young)
They ___ get married.

2 We don't go on expensive holidays. (be rich)
We ___ go on expensive holidays.

3 I didn't have breakfast. (get up late)
I ___ have breakfast.

4 She didn't pass the exam. (work hard)
She ___ pass the exam.

.../4

2 Complete the sentences with one word.

I don't like big cities because there are ⁰*too* many people. There's also too ¹___ pollution and ²___ enough clean air. I think there are too ³___ buildings and there aren't ⁴___ parks.

.../4

3 Complete the words.

0 Is there *any*thing in this bag?

1 I can't find my watch. I've looked every___.

2 The film was boring. ___body enjoyed it.

3 This shop is fantastic. I like every___ in it!

4 I think there's ___thing in my shoe.

5 The school is closed. Every___ has gone home.

6 I'd like to go ___where hot for my holiday.

.../6

Vocabulary (14 marks)

4 Complete the words.

0 How *deep* is this pool? What's its *depth*?

1 What's the s___ of the train? How f___ is it?

2 How h___ is the building? What's its h___?

3 What's the w___ of the river? How w___ is it?

4 What's the l___ of the bridge? How l___ is it?

.../8

5 Write the correct place in town.

0 buy a book? *bookshop*

1 see a painting?

2 post a letter?

3 buy some food?

4 go swimming?

5 drink a coffee?

6 borrow a book?

.../6

Phrases/Use your English (12 marks)

6 Look at the jumbled conversation. Number the lines in the correct order.

☐ a) Yes, very stupid!

1 b) Hi, Jerry. I'm a bit lost!

☐ c) Oh great. 'Flicks' is just opposite my block of flats.

☐ d) Sorry. Can you see anything? I mean, a shop or a park?

☐ e) Oh dear! Where are you? I suppose that's a stupid question.

☐ f) Yes, a cinema called 'Flicks'.

.../5

7 Complete with words and phrases from the box.

• welcome • miss it • turn left • past • Sorry to
• along • Take • Excuse me

A: ⁰ *Excuse me*. How do I get to the post office?

B: ¹___ this road and then go ²___ Chester Road. Go ³___ the bank and then you'll see it.

A: Thanks.

B: You're ⁴___.

A: ⁵___ bother you, can you tell me where the station is?

B: No problem. Go down the road, then ⁶___. You can't ⁷___!

.../7

🎧 LISTEN AND CHECK YOUR SCORE	
Grammar	.../14
Vocabulary	.../14
Phrases/Use your English	.../12
Total	**.../40**

4a I haven't seen the sun for weeks.

Grammar Present perfect simple with *for* and *since*
Vocabulary Collocations with *make* and *do*

Get started

1 Would you like to study abroad for a year? Why?/Why not?

Read

2 🎧 4 01 Listen and read the school webpage. Which subjects are a problem for Martin?

Comprehension

3 Answer true (T), false (F) or doesn't say (DS).

1 Martin is from London. *F*
2 He prefers California to London.
3 He likes the British weather.
4 Maths and Science are different at his new school.
5 He doesn't enjoy French.

| home | year 11 | news | new students |

This term we welcome new student Martin Blake to Year 11. Let's do our best to help him settle in quickly.

Martin comes all the way from the USA and will be with us until next summer. Jodie and Sally interviewed him for us.

How long have you been in London and what do you think of it so far?

I've been here for about a month now. It feels like much longer. To be honest, I didn't like it much when I first arrived. It was so cold and wet, after California! But I've changed my mind since then. I think London is amazing. And since I started at this school, I've made some friends. That makes a big difference.

What do you miss most about California?

My friends mostly, but since I left they've been great – we chat online a lot. And the weather. It feels like I haven't seen the sun for weeks, well, not the Californian sun, anyway! Oh, and I also miss the beach – I haven't been near a surfboard since I left California!

How do the lessons here compare with back home? Do you do the same subjects?

Things like Maths and Science are pretty much the same, but I have problems with French. I've only studied it for about a year so everybody's much better than me. I make loads of mistakes. And I need to do more work on my British history!

Vocabulary: Collocations with *make* and *do*

4a 🎧 Listen and repeat. Then find six of the expressions in the webpage on page 42.

do our best

- do a subject • do nothing/something
- do some exercise • do some/the shopping
- do your best
- do your homework/some work/the housework
- make a decision • make a difference
- make a drink/a cake/a sandwich/a meal
- make a mess • make a mistake
- make a noise • make an appointment (with)
- make friends (with) • make (some) money

b Replace the <u>underlined</u> words with the correct form of expressions from Exercise 4a.

1 We have <u>become friends</u> with our new neighbours. *made friends*
2 Congratulations, your hard work <u>changed the situation</u>.
3 I will <u>do everything I can</u>.
4 I've <u>arranged to see</u> the doctor.
5 We weren't sure, but now we've <u>decided</u>.
6 I need to <u>earn some cash</u>.
7 Jack's <u>studying</u> Art History at college.
8 Can you <u>go to the shops and buy some food</u>?

Grammar

Present perfect simple with *for* and *since*

I**'ve been** here **for** about a month.
I **haven't seen** the sun **for** weeks.
I**'ve changed** my mind **since** then.
Since I started at this school, I**'ve made** some friends.

Complete the rules with *for* or *since*.

We use ¹___ to talk about a period of time.
We use ²___ to talk about a point in the past.

Practice

5 Put the words and phrases in the lists.

- 6 p.m. • a few minutes • ages
- half an hour • we started at this school
- I was twelve • last July • a long time
- six months • 2000 • my birthday
- New Year's Eve • this morning
- three seconds • two weeks • I got up
- yesterday • a thousand years • the spring
- a day

for	since
a few minutes	*6 p.m.*

6 Read the situations and write two sentences for each one. Use the present perfect form of the verbs with *for* and *since*.

1 Tom and Sylvie got married in 2010. (be)
   They've been married for … years.
   They've been married since 2010.
2 Jackie had her first pair of glasses when she was eight. She's fifteen now. (wear)
3 The last time I saw Ben was at his birthday party three months ago. (not see)
4 Cathy and Ted met on their first day of college. That was two years ago. (know)
5 The last time I had a break was at eleven o'clock. It's half past three now. (not have)
6 Della has flu. It's Friday. She became ill on Saturday. (have)

Speak

7a Ask and answer the questions in pairs. Note down your partner's answers.

- Where do you live?
- How long have you lived there?
- What's your favourite band?
- When did you first like him/her/them?
- What's your favourite TV programme?
- When did you first watch it?
- What's your least favourite food?
- When did you last eat it?

b Now tell the class about your partner.

Nikos lives in/at … He's lived there for/since …

Extra practice

▶ For more practice, go to page 54.

4b You've been talking for ages.

Grammar   Present perfect continuous with *for* and *since*

Vocabulary Phrasal verbs with *look*

Dialogue

1 🎧 **Listen and read. Why did Jodie need to speak to Martin?**

> **Martin:** Hi, Jodie.
>
> **Jodie:** Hi, Martin, at last! You've been talking on the phone for ages.
>
> **Martin:** Oh sorry. How long have you been trying?
>
> **Jodie:** Since five o'clock. Have you been talking to the States?
>
> **Martin:** Yes, I have, but I haven't been talking to the same person for three hours! The last one was Sophie.
>
> **Jodie:** Who's Sophie? Your girlfriend?
>
> **Martin:** Let's just say she's a friend. She's been diving in Hawaii for a week. It's not fair! Anyway, what's up?
>
> **Jodie:** It's about that concert at the Brixton Academy next month. Luke and I have been searching online for tickets since lunchtime and …
>
> **Martin:** Don't tell me you've got some!
>
> **Jodie:** Yes, we have, but they're £30 each. What do you think?
>
> **Martin:** Well, I've been saving for a bike since I arrived, but that can wait – I'm in!
>
> **Jodie:** Great. We're on it!

Phrases
• at last! • for ages • Let's just say … • It's about …
• Don't tell me … • I'm in! • We're on it!

Comprehension

2 Choose the correct options.

1 Martin has had **one conversation / several conversations**
2 Sophie is **Martin's / Jodie's** friend.
3 Jodie wanted to tell Martin about a **holiday / concert**.
4 Jodie and Luke **are looking for / have found** some tickets.
5 Martin is saving for a **ticket / bike**.

Vocabulary: Phrasal verbs with *look*

3a Match the phrases (1–5) to the correct endings (a–e).

1 – d

1 look at	a) something exciting
2 look up	b) something you've lost
3 look forward to	c) a baby
4 look for	d) a picture
5 look after	e) a difficult word in a dictionary

b Complete the sentences with *at*, *up*, *forward to*, *for* or *after*.

1 I don't understand this word. I'm going to look it *up.*
2 I'm looking ___ the concert next week.
3 Wow! Look ___ that sunset!
4 That plant is dying. You don't look ___ it well enough.
5 John's lost his wallet. Can you look ___ it, please?

> **SOLVE IT!**
>
> **4 Look at the dialogue in Exercise 1 again. What time does Jodie speak to Martin?**

Pronunciation: /ɪə/ we're, /eə/ where

5 (4/04) Go to page 58.

Grammar

Present perfect continuous with *for* and *since*
Affirmative
You**'ve been talking** on the phone for ages.
I**'ve been saving** for a bike **since** I arrived.
Negative
I **haven't been talking** to the same person **for** three hours.
Questions
How long **have** you **been trying**?
Have you **been talking** to the States?
Short answers
Yes, I **have**./No, I **haven't**.

Practice

6 Complete the questions and answers. Write the present perfect continuous form of the verbs in brackets or short forms.

1 A: You look tired. How long *have you been travelling* (you/travel)?
   B: We ___ (drive) since six o'clock this morning.
2 A: ___ (Tom/do) his homework this morning?
   B: No, he ___. He ___ (play) basketball since 9 a.m.
3 A: Hi. You look fed up!
   B: You're right, I am. I ___ (stand) at this bus stop for half an hour.
4 A: Look at this mess. What ___ (you/do)?
   B: Sorry. We ___ (sort) out our old clothes for the last two hours.
5 A: How long ___ (Amy/prepare) for the half marathon?
   B: She ___ (train) every morning for weeks now – she's very fit!
6 A: Sorry I'm late. ___ (you/wait) for ages?
   B: No, I ___, don't worry.

7 Complete the postcard. Choose *for* or *since* and write the present perfect continuous form of the verbs.

Hi Martin,
This is the last day of our holiday 😕 I 1 *'ve been carrying* (carry) this postcard around ²**for / since** days, but I haven't had time to write it. There's lots to tell you!
On our second day here I made friends with a girl called Kirstie, and ³**for / since** then we ⁴___ (go) around together. Right now we're in a café on the beach. We ⁵___ (sit) here ⁶**for / since** hours and I've had two ice creams!
Guess what – I'm learning to dive! I ⁷___ (only learn) ⁸**for / since** a week so I'm just a beginner, but Kirstie's really good. She ⁹___ (dive) ¹⁰**for / since** she was twelve.
How's London? What ¹¹___ (you/do) ¹²**for / since** the last time we spoke?
I'll call soon,
Love, Sophie xxx

Listen

8 (4/05) Martin and Emma are at the sports centre. Listen and complete the sentences.

1 Emma has been playing badminton *since she was about eight.*
2 Martin first played basketball ___ ago, when he was ___.
3 Emma has been a member of the sports centre for about ___.
4 She has been playing hockey since ___.
5 Martin has been playing football since ___.

Speak

9 Talk about you. Ask and answer in pairs, then tell the class.

- What's your favourite sport or hobby?
- How did you become interested in it?
- How long have you been doing it?

Write

10 Look at Exercise 7 again. Imagine you are on holiday. Write a postcard to a friend back home. Say what you and your family and friends have been doing.

Extra practice

▶ For more practice, go to page 55.

4c She used to be a Goth.

Grammar	used to
	Echo questions
Function	Show interest

Dialogue

1  Listen and read. Who doesn't like the photo?

Jodie: Hey, have a look at this. Guess who the girl is.

Martin: I've no idea. Why? Who is she?

Jodie: It's our mum when she was fifteen!

Martin: **Is it**? Really?

Jodie: Yes. She **used to** be a Goth.

Martin: **Did she**? That's so cool.

Luke: Cool? I think it's weird.

Martin: **Did** she **use to** wear the make-up and clothes at school?

Jodie: No, she **didn't**. But she and her friends **used to** dress up like this at weekends.

Martin: How amazing!

Jodie: Yes, I know. She says it **used to** take hours to put on her make-up and then take it off again.

Martin: What about your dad?

Jodie: Well, he **didn't use to** dress up like that. But he was in a band!

Martin: **Was he**? Wow! Your parents are so interesting!

Luke: **Are they**? I think they're embarrassing!

Comprehension

2 **Answer the questions in pairs.**

1 Who is the girl in the photo?
  Jodie and Luke's mother
2 How old is she in the photo?
3 Did she look like that every day?
4 Who played in a band?
5 What does Martin think about his friends' parents?
6 Does Luke agree?

Grammar

used to
Affirmative
She **used to** be a Goth.
It **used to** take hours.
Negative
He **didn't use to** dress up like that.
Questions
Did she **use to** wear the make-up and clothes at school?
Short answers
Yes, she **did**./No, she **didn't**.

Practice

3a Complete the questions with the correct form of *used to* and the verbs in brackets.

1 What money _did they use to_ have (they/have) in Italy before the euro?
2 ___ (your grandparents/use) computers at school?
3 What ___ (people/do) before they had mobile phones?
4 ___ (some people/believe) the world was flat, not round?
5 ___ (you/go) to school when you were five?

b Now match the questions (1–5) in Exercise 4a to the answers (a–e). Then complete the answers.

1 – e
a) Yes, they ___. They were frightened of falling off!
b) No, I ___. I started when I was six.
c) They ___ (use) landlines.
d) No, they ___ (not have) anything like that. Just books!
e) They _used to have_ (have) the lira.

Speak and write

4a In pairs, talk about you as a child. Use the topics below and *used to/didn't use to*.

When I was five, I used to love the colour pink. I used to wear pink tops, pink skirts, everything pink but I hate the colour now!

• clothes • food • games • hobbies • TV

b Now write about your partner.

When Tomas was little he used to wear the same hat every day.

Grammar

Echo questions	
Affirmative	
A: She used to be a Goth.	B: **Did she?**
A: He was in a band!	B: **Was he?**
A: You look great.	B: **Do I?**
A: We've made dinner.	B: **Have you?**
Negative	
A: I don't like pizza.	B: **Don't you?**
A: They didn't use to like sport.	B: **Didn't they?**
A: She wasn't very nice.	B: **Wasn't she?**
A: He hasn't got up yet.	B: **Hasn't he?**

5 (4.07) Listen and respond. Complete the echo questions. Then listen and check.

1 _Have_ I? 4 ___ it? 7 ___ she?
2 ___ we? 5 ___ she? 8 ___ they?
3 ___ it? 6 ___ you?

Pronunciation: Rising intonation (to show interest)

6 (4.08) Go to page 58.

Use your English: Show interest

7 (4.09) Listen and repeat. Then practise the conversation in pairs.

A: I didn't go online at all last week.
B: Didn't you? Why not?
A: We had no connection.
B: Really? How awful.

Show interest
Echo questions: *Are/Aren't you? Did/Didn't you?*, etc.
Really?
How awful/exciting/amazing …
Why?/Why not?

8 Practise similar conversations in pairs. Then invent other situations.

1 I'm going to be on TV tonight. (They're showing the football match I went to.)
2 I need some dollars. (I'm going to New York.)
3 I'm not coming to school tomorrow morning. (I'm going to the dentist's.)

Extra practice

For more practice, go to page 55.

SKILLS FOCUS: LISTENING AND SPEAKING

Get started

1 When you need some information, which do you prefer to use – a library or the internet? Why? Tell the class.

Read

2 Read the online problem page. What are Ned's two choices?

IN A FIX?

Here's your chance
     to share your problems and say what you think.

Home   About us   Stories

My friend and I often copy stuff from the internet for our homework. Basically we just change some words round to make it look a bit different. I know we shouldn't, but I never really understand why. If the information is correct, why is it wrong to copy it? Anyway, the teachers have caught her, but not me. I actually got a really good mark and she's in big trouble. I don't know how or why it happened because we both use the same websites. We've been doing it for ages! Obviously I've felt a bit bad since it happened, but what can I do? My friend says she won't tell on me and nobody else knows. The thing is, we aren't the only people who do it. I don't really know what to do.

Ned, Oxford

▶ I don't think you should do anything. What's the point? It just means two people get into trouble instead of one. And as you say, everyone does it!   *timbo, Sheffield*

▶ I think you should explain everything to your teacher and talk it through. You shouldn't get into trouble if you're honest about it this time and you don't do it again.   *northernboy, Leeds*

▶ I agree with you, Ned. I don't think it's wrong to copy from the Net. But it IS wrong to abandon your friends! That's why I think you should tell your teacher. Go on, you know I'm right. ☺   *amy15, Lincoln*

Comprehension

3 **Match the beginnings (1–5) to the correct endings (a–e) to make true sentences.**

1 – d

1 Ned's friend has been cheating for some time
2 The teachers have caught her,
3 *timbo* thinks Ned should do nothing,
4 *northernboy* thinks Ned has done wrong
5 *amy15* thinks Ned should do something

a) and he thinks he should tell a teacher.
b) but the other two don't agree.
c) because his friend is in trouble.
d) and Ned has been doing the same.
e) but they haven't caught him.

Speak

4 **Ned says, 'If the information is correct, why is it wrong to copy it?' What do you think? Did Ned do anything wrong? What about his friend? Discuss with your partner, then tell the class.**

5 **Work in pairs. What do you think Ned should do? Why? Tell your partner.**

Write

6 **Read the advice in Exercise 2 again. Then write your advice to Ned. Give reasons.**

I think/don't think you should …

Listen

LISTENING TIP: LISTEN FOR KEY WORDS

Listen to the words which are stressed. These are the key words and they tell you the most important information. Now do Exercise 7.

7a **Listen to the conversation. Complete the missing words and say who is speaking (Mr Benson or Ned).**

1 You know, the *History* project. *Ned*
2 That was ___.
3 Chrissy and I did it ___.
4 But Chrissy just ___ from ___.
5 I did the ___ thing.
6 Did you ___ it?

b **What do you think Mr Benson is going to do?**

8 **Listen to Ned and Chrissy. What is going to happen tomorrow? Do you think it is fair?**

Speak your mind!

SPEAKING TIP: STRESS THE IMPORTANT WORDS

Try to stress the most important words in each sentence. Now do Exercise 9.

9 **Work in pairs. Read the situations (A–D) and discuss the questions (1–3). Then tell the class what you think.**

A Sam took his friend's homework out of his bag and copied it. His friend didn't know.
B Bella's dad did her Maths homework for her while she was watching TV.
C Frankie showed Jack his exam answers while the teacher wasn't looking.
D David's mother helped him with his Geography homework and checked his work.

1 Who was cheating?
2 Who should get into trouble?
3 Whose behaviour was the worst?

Grammar (20 marks)

1 Complete with the present perfect simple form of the verbs. Then choose the correct options.

0 My mum *has been* ill (be) for / since last week.

1 It___ (not rain) **for / since** a week.

2 I___ (not see) him **for / since** a long time.

3 Anne ___ (live) in her flat **for / since** July.

4 They ___ (not visit) us **for / since** my birthday.

.../8

2 Write sentences. Use the present perfect continuous form of the verbs and *for* or *since*.

0 I/save/for a new phone/ages

I've been saving for a new phone for ages.

1 We/cook/4 o'clock

2 They/search/for information online/hours

3 Henry/playing/computer games/lunchtime

4 you/wait/a long time?

.../4

3 Complete the sentences with the correct form of *used to*.

0 My parents *used to live* (live) in London when they were children.

1 Dad ___ (play) football in school.

2 What ___ (you/wear) when you were eight?

3 I ___ (not like) make-up, but I do now.

4 My brother ___ (cry) a lot when he was a baby.

.../4

4 Write the echo questions for these statements.

0 I've just found some money! *Have you?*

1 We're going on holiday tomorrow!

2 Anna didn't go to school yesterday.

3 I live in Manchester.

4 It wasn't very funny.

.../4

Vocabulary (11 marks)

5 Choose the correct options.

0 Don't make / do a noise.

1 He hasn't **made / done** a decision yet.

2 I'll **make / do** an appointment with the vet.

3 In fact, I'm **doing / making** nothing.

4 I'm going to **do / make** a course.

5 She should **make / do** some exercise.

6 My brother **made / did** a mess in his bedroom.

7 Will you **do / make** a cake on Friday?

.../7

6 Complete the extracts from a dictionary.

0 look *at* : to turn your eyes towards something or someone in order to see them

1 look ___ : to do things to make sure that someone or something is safe and well (same meaning as *take care of*)

2 look ___ : to use your eyes to find something

3 look ___ : to find information in a book, on a computer, etc.

4 look ___ : to think about something exciting that is going to happen

.../4

Phrases/Use your English (9 marks)

7 Complete with phrases from the box.

• Don't tell me, • We're on it! • Let's just say
• for ages. • I'm in! • It's about • at last!

A: Pete, ⁰*at last!* I've been looking for you ¹___

B: ²___ you've won something!

A: ³___ I've had a bit of luck.

B: Well. Come on, tell me.

A: I'm in the final of an online game. I need help for the second round. ⁴___ sport. Can you help me?

B: Yes! ⁵___

A: Great. ⁶___

.../6

8 Number the lines of the conversation in the correct order.

☐ a) She's the detective. She studied drama.

☐ b) Are you? What are you going to see?

☐ c) Really? Who's she playing?

☐ d) Did you? Why don't you come with me?

7 e) I'm going to the theatre tonight.

☐ f) Did she? I did drama at university, too.

☐ g) *Murder Mystery*, my sister's in the play.

.../3

LISTEN AND CHECK YOUR SCORE	
Grammar	.../20
Vocabulary	.../11
Phrases/Use your English	.../9
Total	**.../40**

Skills Revision

Read

1 Read the text about Anna's Eco School. Find the <u>underlined</u> words. What do they mean?

1 survey – a questionnaire or project

ANNA'S ECO SCHOOL

ABOUT	BLOG	CONTACT

At our school we have learnt that everybody can do something to help the environment. My class did a ¹**survey** on how much rubbish we throw away every day. We checked all the rubbish bins in the school. You can't imagine how much waste 2,500 ²**pupils** and 150 teachers can produce! There was far too much plastic, paper and even uneaten food. And all that rubbish went to landfill sites. So we decided to take action!

We ³**set up** a school recycling scheme. Everybody does something, teachers and students. We put plastic boxes with ⁴**stickers** next to the bins in all the classrooms and in the school yard. The stickers tell you what type of rubbish you must put into the boxes. At the end of the week someone from each class empties the boxes. Then we send all the rubbish to a recycling ⁵**plant**. Since we started we have been sending 187 kg less paper to the landfill sites every week! What do you do at your school?

2 Answer true (T), false (F), or doesn't say (DS).

0 Anna is writing about a school survey. *T*

1 Anna's class looked at the contents of all the school bins.

2 All the school rubbish went to a big hole in the ground.

3 Only the students recycle rubbish.

4 You get a sticker every time you use a recycling box.

5 Today, pupils at the school don't throw away food.

Listen

3 🎧 (4/14) Listen to a London bus tour guide talking about a famous street, The Strand. Listen for key words and complete the notes.

0 The Strand is one of London's *oldest* roads.

1 'Strand' means river ___ in old English.

2 Today Somerset House is an ___ and ___ centre.

3 On the left is Waterloo ___.

4 The Savoy is a ___ for the rich and famous.

5 There are over ___ theatres in London's West End.

Write

4 Write about a famous street in your country. Write three paragraphs. Start each paragraph with a topic sentence:

1 The most famous street in town

2 Things to see and do there

3 How to get there

NOW I CAN		
Read	identify specific information in a text.	☐
Listen	understand a tour guide and complete notes.	☐
Write	write a short description of a place.	☐

Extra practice

Unit 1

Lesson 1a

1 Put the instruments in the correct lists.

• cello • clarinet • drums • flute • keyboard
• piano • saxophone • trumpet • violin

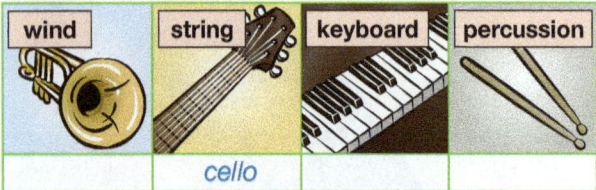

wind	string	keyboard	percussion
	cello		

2 Choose the correct options.

1 **A:** What are you planning for the summer?
   B: We'll / **'re going to** go camping.
2 **A:** The sky is very dark.
   B: Yes, it'll / 's going to rain.
3 **A:** I like that T-shirt.
   B: Will you / Are you going to buy it?
4 **A:** Let's have lunch.
   B: OK, I'll / 'm going to see what's in the fridge.
5 **A:** Where are they going?
   B: The cinema. They'll see / 're going to see
   Mr Bean.
6 **A:** I need some help with my homework.
   B: Why don't you ask Tim? I'm sure he'll / 's
   going to help you.

Lesson 1b

1 Tick (✓) the correct sentences. Correct the
wrong ones. Use *going to* or *will*.

1 Have a look in my diary. What time is Sarah
   arriving? ✓
2 You need a warm coat. ~~It's snowing~~ later.
   It's going to snow.
3 Maths is so hard! I'm probably failing the exam
   next week.
4 I don't like that kind of film. I'm not going to
   the cinema.
5 Don't run across the road. You're having an
   accident.
6 I like John. Is he coming to your party?
7 Go to bed early. You're feeling better
   tomorrow.
8 Sheena is training hard. She's cycling in a
   competition next week.

2 Complete with phrases from the box.

• is playing • at eight o'clock • 'll be good
• ~~fancy going~~ • on 3rd November
• the youth club

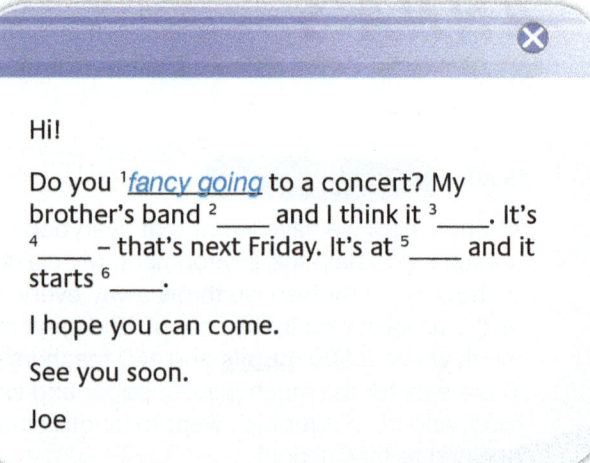

Hi!

Do you ¹*fancy going* to a concert? My
brother's band ²____ and I think it ³____. It's
⁴____ – that's next Friday. It's at ⁵____ and it
starts ⁶____.

I hope you can come.

See you soon.

Joe

Lesson 1c

1a Write sentences to compare these things.
Use the adjectives in brackets and your
opinions.

1 a day at the beach/a day in a city (relaxing,
   exciting)
   *A day at the beach is much more relaxing than
   a day in a city, but it isn't as exciting.*
2 a pizza/a salad (expensive, healthy)
3 a bicycle/a car (cheap, comfortable)
4 English/my language (difficult, beautiful)

b Write your opinions with the superlative form
of the adjectives in brackets.

1 school subject (easy, interesting)
   *Maths is the easiest subject and Geography is
   the most interesting.*
2 animal (intelligent, friendly)
3 day of the week (good, bad)
4 food (delicious, cheap)

Unit 2

Lesson 2a

1 **Read the situations and write sentences. Use the present perfect simple and *just*, *yet*, *already* or *never*.**

1 Jack's nervous about his trip to London. (go/to the UK before)
He's never been to the UK before.

2 John's room looks great. (tidy/it)

3 Emma isn't going to the cinema with her friends. (see/the film twice)

4 Rosie is going to be late for school. (not wake up)

5 My parents are relaxing in the sitting room. (get/home from work)

6 I'm very hungry. (not have/breakfast)

7 John doesn't need to borrow that book. (read/it)

8 The children on the beach are very excited. (see/the sea before)

Lesson 2b

1 **Complete the sentences with relationship words and phrases.**

1 Steve is my friend. I *get* *on* well with him.

2 My brother is going ____ ____ a really nice girl.

3 They don't look happy. I think they're having an ____ .

4 Ben isn't her boyfriend now. They ____ ____ last week.

5 Jane is very happy these days. I think she has fallen ____ ____ ____ somebody!

6 They were married for ten years, but then they got ____ .

2 **Complete the conversations. Use the past simple or present perfect simple form of the verbs, or short answers.**

meet

A: [1]*Have you ever met* (you/ever) a famous person?

B: Yes, I [2]____ . About ten years ago, I [3]____ Paul McCartney!

A: Where [4]____ (you) him?

B: In a music shop.

break

A: [5]____ (you/ever) a bone?

B: Yes, I [6]____ . I [7]____ my toe last year.

A: How [8]____ (you) it?

B: I was playing football, in the wrong shoes.

Lesson 2c

1a **Complete the sentences with *who*, *which*, *where* or *whose*.**

1 Luke is a man *who* doesn't often get angry.

2 I've just seen the film ____ you told me about.

3 I don't believe the stories ____ my brother tells.

4 I'd like to live in a place ____ it never rains.

5 She's the girl ____ father was on TV last night.

6 Where's the CD ____ we were listening to?

7 I'm going to invite the people ____ I like.

8 Here's somebody ____ wants to speak to you.

9 They are the boys ____ I met at the youth club.

10 This is the house ____ my grandmother lives.

b **Which sentences don't need a relative pronoun? Write the new sentences.**

2 I've just seen the film you told me about.

Unit 3

Lesson 3a

1 **Look at the information. Then complete the conversation with the words from the box.**

> • deep • depth • height • high • length
> • long • ~~old~~ • wide • width

1,149 m

49 m

Sydney Harbour Bridge: opened 1932

134 m   12 m   12 m

A: How [1]*old* is the Sydney Harbour Bridge?

B: No idea! Let's look on the internet. ... Well, it opened in 1932.

A: OK, and how [2]____ is it?

B: Its [3]____ is 1,149 metres.

A: Right. What about its [4]____ ?

B: It says here the bridge is 134 metres [5]____ .

A: Great. And how [6]____ is it?

B: Its [7]____ is 49 metres.

A: I need to know the [8]____ of the water, too.

B: It's twelve metres [9]____ at both ends of the bridge.

2 Read the situations and write sentences with *too ... to* or *(not) ... enough to*.

1 I'm tired. I can't stay awake for the film.
   I'm too tired to stay awake for the film.
2 It's cold. Don't go out without a coat.
3 I don't get up early. I never catch the bus.
4 We were late. We didn't get tickets.
5 He is clever. He understands the problem.
6 He isn't very old. He doesn't go to school.

Lesson 3b

1 Look at the map on page 34 and write directions.

1 Go left out of the tourist information centre and go along Princess Street. The supermarket is on the left, it's opposite the music shop.

from	to
1 the tourist information centre	the supermarket
2 the library	the park
3 the cinema	the sports centre
4 the pharmacy	the art gallery

Lesson 3c

1 Read the situations and write sentences with *there is/are* and *too many/much* or *not enough*.

1 This party is awful. (noisy people)
   There are too many noisy people.
2 I'm going to the shops. (food)
3 This road is always very busy. (cars)
4 I don't understand. (information)
5 We can't sit down. (chairs)
6 The streets are dirty. (rubbish)

2 Complete the sentences with *some/any/no/every* and *one/thing/body/where*.

1 I don't know *anybody* who lives in London.
2 Oh no! I've dropped my glass. There's milk ____.
3 Listen! ____ is calling your name!
4 Tom is very popular, ____ likes him.
5 I can't find my mobile ____.
6 They've all gone out. There's ____ at home.
7 Let's find ____ peaceful for our picnic.
8 Ouch! There's ____ in my eye!

Unit 4

Lesson 4a

1 Complete the sentences so that they mean the same.

1 I haven't seen Jim since 10 a.m. It's 12 p.m. now.
   I *haven't seen Jim for* two hours.
2 We moved here in 2009 and we still live here.
   We ____ 2009.
3 The last time we saw them was in July.
   We ____ July.
4 They first met when they were at primary school.
   They have known each other ____.
5 They got married in 1990 and they are still married.
   They ____ years.
6 He went to sleep ten hours ago. He's still asleep.
   He ____ ten hours.

2 Complete the sentences with *make* or *do*. Then match the statements (1–5) to the replies (a–e).

1 – d

1 You need to be smart. A good haircut will *make* a difference.
2 I'm really nervous! I don't want to ____ a mistake.
3 Dad has asked me to ____ some work for him. I'm going to paint the door.
4 When are you going to ____ the shopping?
5 Which subjects are you going to ____ next year?

a) You'll be fine. Just ____ your best.
b) Later. I have to ____ my homework now.
c) I'm not sure. I can't ____ a decision!
d) You're right. I'll ____ an appointment at the hairdresser.
e) OK, but please don't ____ a mess.

Lesson 4b

1 Look at the picture and information. Then write sentences about Gina. Use the present perfect continuous form of the verbs in the box and *for* or *since*.

| • support • ~~learn~~ • go • wear • play |

1 Gina has been learning Italian for a year.

1 first Italian lesson: a year ago
2 started playing the guitar: age fourteen
3 started wearing glasses: three years ago
4 first day at Manor School: age eleven
5 became Manchester United supporter: five years ago

Lesson 4c

1 Ryan is talking to his grandfather. Complete the conversation with the correct form of *used to* or short answers.

Ryan: Where ¹*did you use to go* (you/go) to school?

Grandfather: In London. I ² ____ (travel) to school by bus. We ³ ____ (not have) a car. We ⁴ ____ (go) by bus or Tube, or we ⁵ ____ (walk).

Ryan: I suppose you ⁶ ____ (not use) computers at work, either.

Grandfather: You're right. I saw my first computer when I was about thirty!

Ryan: ⁷ ____ (you/have) a TV?

Grandfather: Yes, we ⁸ ____. I'm not 100, you know!

2 Look at the responses and complete the conversations with the correct form of the verbs.

1 A: *I didn't go out* (not go out) last weekend.
   B: Didn't you? How boring!

2 A: ____ (win) £2,000 in a competition.
   B: Has she? How exciting!

3 A: ____ (break up).
   B: Have they? How sad!

4 A: ____ (not go) to school tomorrow.
   B: Aren't you? How nice!

5 A: ____ (not tell) us his name.
   B: Hasn't he? How strange!

6 A: ____ (not be) a very good match.
   B: Wasn't it? How annoying!

Word bank

Welcome

Welcome a

Personality adjectives
• annoying • bad-tempered • big-headed
• bossy • clever • cute • easy-going
• friendly • funny • generous • hard-working
• helpful • honest • kind • lazy • loyal
• mean • polite • quiet • rude • shy • tidy
• unfriendly • untidy

Welcome b

House and furniture
Rooms • bathroom • bedroom
• dining room • hall • kitchen • living room
• study

Parts of a house • balcony • basement
• ceiling • chimney • door • downstairs
• floor • garage • garden • gate • landing
• loft • roof • stairs • steps • upstairs
• wall • window

Fittings • bath • cooker • dishwasher
• fridge • shower • sink • toilet
• washbasin • washing machine

Furniture • armchair • bed • bookcase
• carpet • CD player • chair
• chest of drawers • clock • computer
• cupboard • curtains • desk
• DVD player • lamp • mirror • plant • shelf
• sofa • table • television (TV) • wardrobe
• wastepaper bin

Welcome c

Jobs
• actor • artist • beautician • builder
• carpenter • cashier • chef • dentist
• detective • director • doctor • electrician
• engineer • farmer • firefighter • hairdresser
• housewife • journalist • mechanic • model
• musician • nurse • pilot • plumber
• police officer • politician • receptionist
• reporter • secretary • shop assistant
• ski instructor • sound engineer • taxi driver
• teacher • TV presenter • vet
• waiter/waitress

Welcome d

Clothes
• baseball cap • boots • cardigan • coat
• dress • hat • hoodie • jacket • jeans
• leggings • sandals • shirt • shoes
• shorts • skirt • socks • sweater
• sweatshirt • tights • top • trainers
• trousers • T-shirt

Accessories
• belt • gloves • pocket • scarf • tie • zip

Styles
• baggy • casual • sleeveless • smart
• tight

Patterns
• checked • flowery • patterned • plain
• spotted • striped

Unit 1

Lesson 1a

Types of music
• classical • country and western • folk
• heavy metal • hip-hop • jazz • Latin
• pop • R & B • rap • reggae • rock • soul
• techno

Unit 2

Lesson 2a

Household jobs
• do the cleaning • do the cooking
• do the ironing • do the shopping
• do the washing • do the washing-up
• do the vacuuming • empty the dishwasher
• lay the table • make breakfast/lunch/dinner
• make the bed • take the rubbish out
• tidy your room • wash the car

Lesson 2c

Family
• grandmother • grandfather • grandparents
• mother (mum) • father (dad) • parents
• brother • sister • son • daughter
• husband • wife • aunt • uncle • nephew
• niece • cousin • an only child

Unit 3

Lesson 3a

Transport
- bike • boat • bus • car • caravan
- coach • ferry • helicopter • lorry
- minibus • moped • motorbike • plane
- scooter • ship • taxi • train • tram
- underground (Tube) • van

Lesson 3b

Places in town
- art gallery • bank • bookshop
- bus stop • café • car park • cashpoint
- cinema • computer shop • factory
- hospital • hotel • library • market
- museum • music shop • newsagent
- office • park • petrol station • pharmacy
- police station • post office • restaurant
- school • shop • shopping centre • sports
centre • square • station • supermarket
- swimming pool • theatre
- tourist information centre • town hall
- travel agent • zoo

Pronunciation

Unit 1 Lesson 1b

🎧 1/06 **Exercise 5** /eɪ/ gr**ea**t, /aɪ/ l**i**ke

a **Listen and repeat.**

/eɪ/ great   /aɪ/ like

b **Listen. Is the sound /eɪ/ (1) or /aɪ/ (2)? Listen again and repeat.**

great *1* like *2* afraid ages arrange baby birthday decide diary fine five OK I'd invite late make my place stay why

c **Listen and repeat. Then practise saying the sentences.**

1 What time did you write in your diary?
2 I'm afraid five o'clock is too late in the day.
3 I'd like to invite you to stay on my birthday.

Unit 2 Lesson 2c

🎧 2/08 **Exercise 7** /æ/ f**a**mily, /ɑː/ f**a**ther

a **Listen and repeat.**

/æ/ family   /ɑː/ father

b **Put the words in the correct lists. Then listen and check.**

adult anxious **are** **a**rgument **au**nt exam family father hand have last married matter natural p**ar**t p**ar**ty st**ar**t

/æ/	/ɑː/
adult	*are*

c **Listen and repeat. Then practise saying the sentences.**

1 Dad had an argument with my aunt.
2 Let's relax and have a party.
3 I can't do the exam but my father can.

Unit 3 Lesson 3b

🎧 3/06 **Exercise 6 Sentence stress and rhythm**

a **Listen and underline the words that are stressed. Then listen and repeat.**

1 Can you <u>tell</u> me the <u>way</u> to the <u>hospital,</u> <u>please</u>?
2 How do I get to the park?
3 Turn left and go straight on.

b **Practise saying the sentences. Replace the words in bold with the words in brackets.**

1 Can you tell me the way to the **hospital**, please? (post office/music shop/library)
2 How do I get to the **park**? (bank/zoo/square)
3 Turn left and **go straight on**. (then turn right/it's on the right)

Unit 4 Lesson 4b

🎧 4/04 **Exercise 5** /ɪə/ w**e're**, /eə/ wh**ere**

a **Listen and repeat.**

/ɪə/	/eə/
we're	where
here	hair
fear	fair
dear	dare
really	rarely
ear	air

b **Underline the /ɪə/ sounds and circle the /eə/ sounds. Then listen and check.**

A: Are we <u>nearly</u> th**e**re?
B: No, we're nowhere near.

A: Look! Her hair isn't really fair!
B: Ssh, dear. Don't stare!

A: Come and sit here, Claire.
B: Where? On that chair?

c **Practise the conversations in Exercise 5b in pairs.**

Unit 4 Lesson 4c

🎧 4/08 **Exercise 6 Rising intonation (to show interest)**

a **Listen to the six exchanges. Which responses show interest?**

1 A: I don't feel very well.
  B: Don't you?
2 A: It was brilliant.
  B: Was it?
3 A: John's got a new bike.
  B: Has he?
4 A: I can speak German.
  B: Can you?
5 A: I didn't go to school yesterday.
  B: Didn't you?
6 A: Kate hasn't arrived yet.
  B: Hasn't she?

b **Listen and repeat the responses. Sound interested each time.**

Word list

Unit 1

Lesson 1a

Types of music and musical instruments
cello
clarinet
double bass
drums
flute
guitar
keyboard
piano
saxophone
trumpet
violin
voice

portfolio
record of achievements

Lesson 1b
babysitting
(He) can/can't make it.
Hang on.
What's up?

Lesson 1c

Adjectives of opinion
amazing
awesome
awful
boring
complicated
confusing
disappointing
dull
enjoyable
excellent
exciting
frightening
funny
interesting
sad
scary
violent

absolute favourite
special effects
superhero
without a doubt

Lesson 1d
backstage
be into (something)
cash
choir
choral
compete
fort
fusion
gear
marquee
perform
rehearse
semi-finals (of a competition)
take place
tough

Unit 2

Lesson 2a
calculator
charity shop
good for you!
Ha ha, very funny
How do you know?
sort out
you do that

Lesson 2b

Relationship words and phrases
argue/have an argument (with)
ask somebody out
be friends (with)
be/get annoyed (with)
break up (with)
fall in love (with)
fall out (with)
get divorced (from)
get engaged/married (to)
get on well (with)
go out (with)
make up

it's driving me mad
shocked

Lesson 2c

Family
daughter/son-in-law
fiancée/fiancé
married
mother/father-in-law
single (person)
sister/brother-in-law
stepmother/father
stepsister/brother

affect
anxious
attention
freedom
leader
(an) only child
peacemaker
share
trust
unimportant

Lesson 2d
a couple of
blast
drop out
guess what
hero-worship (v)
spare
taste (in music, etc.)
mean (= unkind)
look forward to
It's up to (you).
That's just it.

Unit 3

Lesson 3a

Adjectives and nouns of measurement

age
big
cost
deep
depth
distance
expensive
far
fast
height
high
length
long
old
size
speed
wide
width

---

avoid
cable car
crowded
double-decker
on foot
rickshaw
sights

Lesson 3b

cross over
I mean, …
I'm a bit lost.
straight on
the (first) turning
what now?

Lesson 3c

Countable and uncountable nouns

air
city
glass
hole
litter
luggage
news
plastic
problem
pollution
rubbish
traffic

---

average
global warming
greenhouse gas
ground
hole

increase
land (n)
landfill site
methane
one third
overseas
poison
recycle
refuse collector
waste (v)

Lesson 3d

appreciate
commentary
cruise
fit
harbour
hero
home-made
illuminated
pirates
skyline
skyscraper
tales
underground
waterways

Unit 4

Lesson 4a

Collocations with *make* and *do*

do a subject
do nothing/something
do some exercise
do some/the shopping
do your best
do your homework/
  some work/the
  housework
make a decision
make a difference
make a drink/a cake/a
  sandwich/a meal
make a mess
make a mistake
make a noise
make an appointment
  (with)
make friends (with)
make (some) money

Californian
mostly
pretty much
settle in
surfboard
to be honest
welcome (v)

Lesson 4b

Phrasal verbs with *look*

look after
look at
look for
look forward to
look up

---

at last!
Don't tell me …
for ages
I'm in!
It's about …
Let's just say …
We're on it!

Lesson 4c

guess
no idea
make-up
take off (clothes, etc.)

Lesson 4d

abandon
as you say
basically
cheat
copy (v)
in (big) trouble
in a fix
instead of
nobody else
obviously
stuff (n)
talk something through
tell on somebody
the thing is, …
What's the point?

Irregular verbs

Infinitive	Past	Past participle
be	was/were	been/gone
beat	beat	beaten
become	became	become
begin	began	begun
bend	bent	bent
break	broke	broken
bring	brought	brought
build	built	built
burn	burnt	burnt
buy	bought	bought
catch	caught	caught
choose	chose	chosen
come	came	come
cost	cost	cost
cut	cut	cut
do	did	done
draw	drew	drawn
dream	dreamt	dreamt
drink	drank	drunk
drive	drove	driven
eat	ate	eaten
fall	fell	fallen
feel	felt	felt
fight	fought	fought
find	found	found
fly	flew	flown
forget	forgot	forgotten
get	got	got
give	gave	given
go	went	gone/been
grow	grew	grown
hang	hung/hanged	hung/hanged
have	had	had
hear	heard	heard
hide	hid	hidden
hit	hit	hit
hold	held	held
hurt	hurt	hurt
keep	kept	kept
know	knew	known
learn	learnt	learnt
leave	left	left
lend	lent	lent

Infinitive	Past	Past participle
light	lit	lit
lose	lost	lost
make	made	made
mean	meant	meant
meet	met	met
pay	paid	paid
put	put	put
read	read /red/	read /red/
ride	rode	ridden
ring	rang	rung
run	ran	run
say	said	said
see	saw	seen
sell	sold	sold
send	sent	sent
shake	shook	shaken
shine	shone	shone
show	showed	shown
shut	shut	shut
sing	sang	sung
sink	sank	sunk
sit	sat	sat
sleep	slept	slept
smell	smelt	smelt
speak	spoke	spoken
spend	spent	spent
spread	spread	spread
stand	stood	stood
steal	stole	stolen
sting	stung	stung
swim	swam	swum
take	took	taken
teach	taught	taught
tear	tore	torn
tell	told	told
think	thought	thought
throw	threw	thrown
understand	understood	understood
wake	woke	woken
wear	wore	worn
win	won	won
write	wrote	written

3A

SPLIT EDITION

LIVE BEAT

WORKBOOK

Rod Fricker

Pearson Education Limited
Edinburgh Gate
Harlow
Essex CM20 2JE
England
and Associated Companies throughout the world.

www.pearsonELT.com

© Pearson Education Limited 2015

The right of Rod Fricker to be identified as author of this Work has been asserted by them in accordance with the Copyright, Designs and Patents Act 1988.

First published 2015

ISBN: 978-1-292-10196-5

Set in Helvetica Neue LT Std 55 Roman 10/14pt

Printed Slovakia by Neografia

Acknowledgements

The publisher would like to thank the following for their kind permission to reproduce their photographs:

(Key: b-bottom; c-centre; l-left; r-right; t-top)

Alamy Images: City Image 93tr, imagebroker 71, Kumar Sriskandan 93/3; DK Images: Jules Selmes 83/3, Neil Setchfield 83/7; John Foxx Images: Images 4 Communication 93/1; Rex Features: Billy Farrell Agency 83/5, David Fisher 83/1; Shutterstock.com: Alan Freed 93/2

Cover images: *Front:* **Shutterstock.com:** Rido

All other images © Pearson Education

Every effort has been made to trace the copyright holders and we apologise in advance for any unintentional omissions. We would be pleased to insert the appropriate acknowledgement in any subsequent edition of this publication.

Illustrated by:

Kathy Baxendale; Robin Lawrie (Beehive Illustration); Sean Longcroft; Pat Murray (Graham-Cameron Illustrations); Eric Smith; James Walmesley (Graham-Cameron Illustrations)

Contents

WELCOME

Vocabulary: Personality adjectives

1 ⭐ **Match the sentences (1–6) to the personality words (a–f).**

1 Debbie borrows my clothes without asking and spends ages in the bathroom. She's really … _c_

2 Mark is always angry. I don't know why he's so … ___

3 Louise is always first in tests and knows all the answers in lessons. She's really … ___

4 Paula always makes us laugh. She's very … ___

5 Tom is always willing to do jobs around the house. He's very … ___

6 Donna's nice but she doesn't say much. She's very … ___

a) funny. d) helpful.

b) quiet. e) bad-tempered.

c) annoying. f) clever.

2 ⭐⭐ **Complete the sentences with the correct personality adjectives.**

1 Frank always says hello and smiles when he meets you. He's very f_riendly_.

2 Belinda always tells people what to do. She's very b_____.

3 Ed never worries about anything and never gets nervous. He's very e_____ -g_____.

4 Gina shares everything with her friends, she even gives away her last sweets. She's very g_____.

5 Liam never does anything. He doesn't do housework and he hates doing exercise. He's very l_____.

6 Rob never says hello or please or thank you. He's very r_____.

7 Sue finds it difficult to talk to people she doesn't know. She's quite s_____.

8 Ursula's room is always a mess. She's very u_____.

Grammar: Present simple and present continuous

3 ⭐ **Match the questions (1–7) to the answers (a–g).**

1 What are you doing? _d_

2 Are you using this pen? ___

3 What's the weather like today? ___

4 What does your dad do? ___

5 Do you know that girl's name? ___

6 What are you studying in History? ___

7 What do you want to do this weekend? ___

a) No, I'm not. You can borrow it if you want.

b) I'd like to go to the cinema.

c) No, I don't. I think she's new.

d) I'm reading a book.

e) It's raining.

f) We're learning about Henry VIII.

g) He's a teacher.

4 ⭐⭐ **Use the prompts to complete the dialogue.**

A: Hi, Mark. [1]_Do you remember_ (you remember) me?

B: … er, Sara?

A: That's right. It's great to see you. [2]_____ (What/you/do) here?

B: [3]_____ (I/wait) for a bus.

A: Yes, but [4]_____ (where/you/go)?

B: Oh, sorry. [5]_____ (I/go) to the sports centre. My brother's there. [6]_____ (He/play) badminton every Saturday.

A: [7]_____ (you/like) sports?

B: Not really. [8]_____ (I/prefer) shopping.

A: Me too.

B: [9]_____ (you/go) shopping now?

A: Yes. Oh look. [10]_____ (The bus/come).

B: Maybe I can meet you later?

A: Yes, that's a great idea. Here's my phone number ….

b

Vocabulary: House and furniture

1 ⭐ **Label the picture. Complete the text with the objects (1–6).**

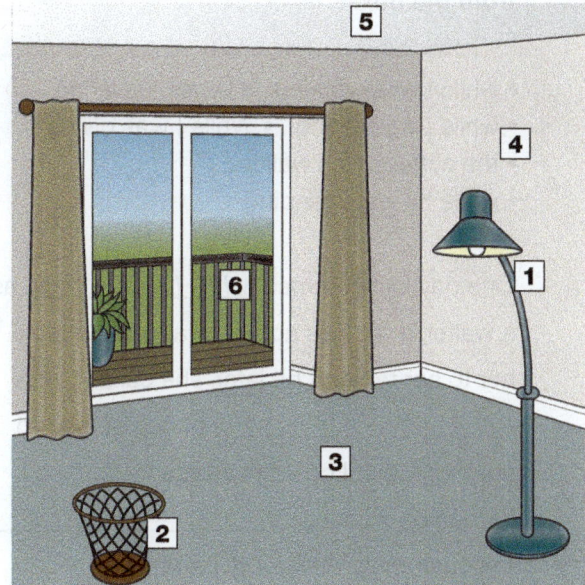

This is my new room. There isn't any furniture in it at the moment. There's just a ¹*lamp* and a ²_____ on the ³_____. I want to paint the ⁴_____ green and the ⁵_____ blue, like the sky. That will look cool. The best thing about my room is that it's got a ⁶_____. I do my homework there when it's warm.

2 ⭐⭐ **Complete the words.**

1 You wash in the b*athroom*.
2 You put your books in the b_____.
3 You keep your clothes in your w_____.
4 You put a c_____ on the floor to walk on.
5 If you have a d_____, you don't need to do the washing-up.
6 My sister always looks at herself in the m_____ before she goes out.
7 In our house, the bedrooms and bathroom are u_____ and the kitchen and living room are d_____.
8 You wash your hands in a w_____, but dishes and pots in the s_____.
9 The f_____ keeps your food cold.
10 We keep the car in the g_____ at night.

Grammar: Countable and uncountable nouns with *some, any, a/an* and *no*

3 ⭐ **Choose the correct options.**

1 There aren't ___ stairs in this house.
   a) any   b) no   c) some

2 Is there ___ mirror in your bedroom?
   a) some   b) a   c) any

3 Great! We haven't got ___ homework this weekend.
   a) some   b) any   c) no

4 It's Monday, but there's ___ school because it's a holiday.
   a) no   b) any   c) a

5 There are ___ interesting photos in this album.
   a) any   b) a   c) some

6 We live in a flat so we haven't got ___ garden.
   a) a   b) no   c) any

7 Why are there ___ books in your bookcase?
   a) any   b) a)   c) no

8 We've got ___ nice, old house.
   a) some   b) a   c) an

4 ⭐⭐ **Complete the dialogue with *a, an, any, some* or *no*.**

Adam: I need to make my bedroom look nice.

Lisa: You could put ¹*some* posters on your walls.

Adam: I haven't got ²_____ posters. No, what I want is ³_____ plant. ⁴_____ interesting, colourful and very big plant. The problem is there are ⁵_____ plant shops near my house.

Lisa: Really? None at all? The garden centre on Park Road is good. They've got ⁶_____ beautiful plants there.

Adam: OK, good idea. Thanks. My mum can take me on Saturday.

Lisa: Can I come? I can help you choose ⁷_____ nice plants.

Adam: Thanks! I could use ⁸_____ help.

C

Vocabulary: Jobs

1 ⭐ **Match the word beginnings (1–5 and 6–10) to the endings (a–e and f–j) to make jobs.**

1 wait	a) el
2 act	b) ist
3 art	c) er
4 electric	d) or
5 mod	e) ian
6 secret	f) ant
7 doct	g) ian
8 shop assist	h) ress
9 wait	i) ary
10 music	j) or

2 ⭐ **Look at the pictures and complete the jobs with one letter in each space.**

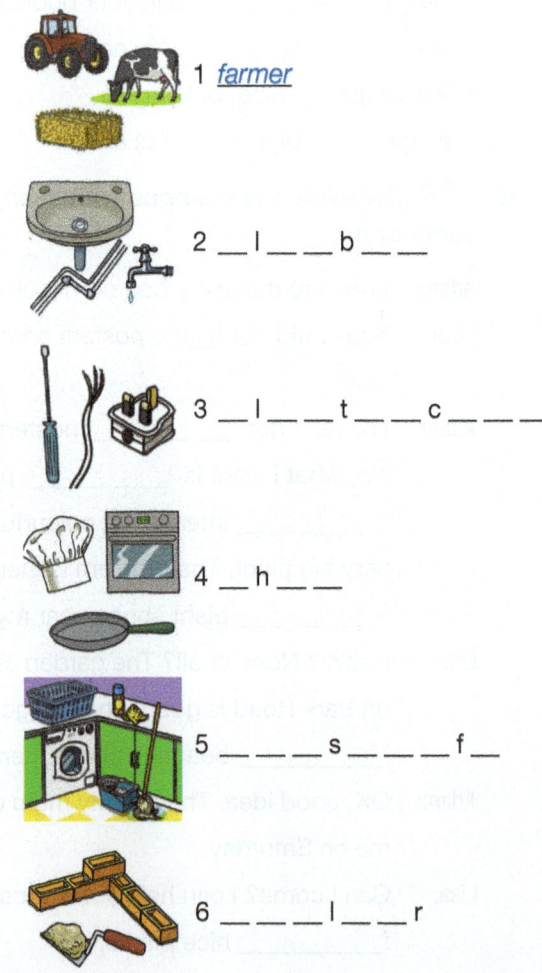

1 *farmer*

2 _ l _ _ _ b _ _ _

3 _ l _ _ _ t _ _ _ c _ _ _ _

4 _ h _ _ _

5 _ _ _ _ s _ _ _ _ f _

6 _ _ _ _ _ l _ _ r

Grammar: Past simple and past continuous; Time markers: *when, while*

3 ⭐ **Complete the text with the phrases from the box.**

- while I was working • When I finished
- while I was taking • While I was giving
- the actress was walking
- while he was standing

One day last summer, [1] *while I was working* as a waiter, a famous actress walked in. I took her to her table. A bit later, she called to me [2] _____ plates of food to another table. I couldn't suddenly stop so I carried on working. [3] _____ the customers their food, I suddenly realised that the actress was standing right behind me. 'I'm waiting,' she said, angrily. I told her that I was busy and turned away. [4] _____ serving the other customers, I turned around and saw that [5] _____ out of the restaurant. My boss was very angry at first but, [6] _____ there, looking at me, all the other customers started clapping and cheering. My boss realised that I was right and she was wrong. I never liked her films anyway!

4 ⭐⭐ **Complete the second sentence so that it has the same meaning as the first.**

1 While I was walking to school, it started to rain.

  I was *walking to school when it started to rain.*

2 I was playing computer games when the electricity went off.

  The electricity _____.

3 The police officer was driving when he saw the bank robbers.

  While the _____.

WELCOME

d

Grammar: *Wh-* questions; Question words

1 ⭐ **Choose the correct options.**

1 '___ dress do you want?' 'The blue one.'

   a) What   b) Which   c) How

2 '___ did you get those shoes?' 'In the new shop in town.'

   a) How much b) Where   c) How long

3 '___ were they?' '£24.99.'

   a) How many b) How much   c) How far

4 '___ are these trainers?' 'They're John's.'

   a) Who   b) Where   c) Whose

5 '___ pairs of shoes have you got?' 'About 15.'

   a) How long b) How much   c) How many

6 '___ do you go shopping for clothes?' 'Every Saturday.'

   a) How often b) How long   c) How far

7 '___ do you like this shop?' 'It's very cheap.'

   a) Why   b) Which   c) Where

8 '___ gave you this shirt?' 'My aunt.'

   a) What   b) Who   c) Whose

2 ⭐⭐ **Complete the questions.**

A: Excuse me. [1]*What* do you do?

B: I'm a teacher.

A: [2]_____ do you work?

B: At St Mark's School in Coventry.

A: [3]_____ away is that?

B: It's about 6 km from here.

A: [4]_____ do you get to work?

B: By car.

A: [5]_____ of car have you got?

B: A Nissan Micra.

A: [6]_____ are your students?

B: They're aged from eleven to eighteen.

A: [7]_____ students are there in the school?

B: About 1,200.

A: [8]_____ do you give homework?

B: Once a week.

Vocabulary: Clothes

3 ⭐ **Look at the picture and match the words (1–11) to the numbers (1–4).**

1 T-shirt	*3*		7 plain	___
2 jumper	___		8 patterned	___
3 gloves	___		9 striped	___
4 dress	___		10 tight	___
5 sleeveless	___		11 spotted	___
6 baggy	___			

4 ⭐⭐ **Label the picture.**

1 b<u>aseball</u> c<u>ap</u>

2 s_____

3 c_____
   s_____

4 b_____

5 p_____

6 z_____

7 j_____

8 s_____

9 s_____

1a I'm going to apply.

Vocabulary: Types of music and musical instruments

1 ⭐ **Rearrange the letters to make types of music.**

MUSIC FESTIVAL
This weekend in the park

Music from all over the world.

We have ¹_jazz_ (zajz), ²_____ (nalit), ³_____ (areegg), ⁴_____ (luso), ⁵_____ (chonte), ⁶_____ (slacislac), ⁷_____ (cork), ⁸_____ (vahye talem), and, from the USA, ⁹_____ (troncyu) and _____ (stewner).

It's free so come and have fun in the sun!

2 ⭐⭐ **Label the picture.**

1 c_ello_	6 t _____
2 d_____	7 c_____
b_____	8 f_____
3 v_____	9 s_____
4 g_____	10 k_____
5 d_____	

Grammar: Future with *going to* and *will*

3 ⭐ **Match the functions from the box to the sentences.**

- plan • ~~intention~~ • promise
- prediction with evidence
- prediction without evidence • decision

1 I'm going to work harder next year. _intention_

2 I don't know this film, but I think you'll enjoy it. _____

3 'There are three tickets left for the concert.' 'Oh, I'll have one.' _____

4 This film is brilliant. It's going to win lots of Oscars. _____

5 I'll give you back your DVD next week. _____

6 We're going to leave at eight o'clock tomorrow morning. _____

4 ⭐⭐ **Complete the sentences with the best form of the words in brackets.**

Tara: Where ¹_will we be_ (we/be) in twenty years' time?

Gina: I've no idea.

Tara: I think ²_____ (you/have) your own business. ³_____ (You/be) a photographer or an artist or something like that. ⁴_____ (You/not/be) rich, but ⁵_____ (you/be) very happy.

Gina: Well, I know something. ⁶_____ (I/not/pass) the Maths exam tomorrow. I don't understand it at all!

5 ★★★ Complete the dialogue with the correct form of the verbs from the box.

> • start • call • think • make • put
> • not get • be • not do

Steve: Hi, Gerry. How are your guitar lessons?

Gerry: Great. I'm quite good now. I ¹*'m going to start* a band.

Steve: Really? Do you know any other musicians?

Gerry: No, but I've got this advert. I ²_____ it on the noticeboard at the music school when I go for my lesson this afternoon.

Steve: Good idea! Hey, I know. I ³_____ your manager. I ⁴_____ you famous but you have to promise me something.

Gerry: What?

Steve: That you ⁵_____ a different manager if you become successful. You know, some big name from the USA.

Gerry: Don't worry! I ⁶_____ anything to upset you. You're my best friend.

Steve: Hey. What ⁷_____ your band? You need a good name.

Gerry: I haven't thought about it. I guess I ⁸_____ of a name when I know who the other members are. Right, I must go. My lesson starts soon.

Steve: OK, see you later.

Grammar summary

Future with *going to*

Affirmative	Negative
I'm **going to work** hard.	I'm **not going to work** hard.
You**'re going to be** late.	You **aren't going to be** late.
He/She/It**'s going to win**.	He/She/It **isn't going to win**.
We**'re going to watch** a film.	We **aren't going to watch** a film.
Questions	**Short answers**
Are you **going to finish** soon?	Yes, I **am**.
Am I **going to be** in the team?	No, I'm **not**.
	Yes, you **are**.
	No, you **aren't**.
Is he/she/it **going to wait** for us?	Yes, he/she/it **is**.
	No, he/she/it **isn't**.
Are we/they **going to leave** soon?	Yes, we/they **are**.
	No, we/they **aren't**.

Note

Use

We use *going to* for plans, intentions and predictions based on present evidence.

Form

We use the correct form of the verb *to be* + *going to* + infinitive without *to*.

Future with *will*

Affirmative

I/You/He/She/It/We/They**'ll (will) be** successful.

Negative

I/You/He/She/It/We/They **won't (will not) live** here in the future.

Questions

Will I/you/he/she/it/we/they **be** rich in the future?

Short answers

Yes, I/you/he/she/it/we/they **will**.
No, I/you/he/she/it/we/they **won't (will not)**.

Note

Use

We use *will* for decisions made at the time of speaking, promises and predictions made without present evidence.

Form

We use *will* + infinitive without *to*. We don't need any other auxiliary verb to make questions and negatives.

1b I'm going out.

Phrases

1 ⭐ **Complete the dialogue with the phrases from the box.**

> • can make it • can't make it • hang on
> • ~~What's up?~~

Jane: Hello, Sally.

Sally: Hi, Jane. ¹*What's up?*

Jane: It's Ruth. She ² _____ on Friday evening. She's looking after her little sister. We'll have to meet on Saturday.

Sally: OK. No, ³ _____ a minute. Saturday's no good for me. I'm going out with Harry. Friday's the only day that I ⁴ _____. Why don't we meet at Ruth's on Friday? We can all look after her little sister.

Jane: That's a good idea!

Grammar: Present continuous for future arrangements

2 ⭐ **Complete the sentences with the correct form of the verbs in brackets.**

1 *I'm going* (I/go) to the dentist on Tuesday afternoon.

2 _____ (Simon/meet) his friend Julie on Wednesday.

3 _____ (Tom and I/play) tennis later today.

4 _____ (My mum and dad/have) a party on Friday.

5 _____ (What/you/do) after school today?

6 _____ (We/not go) on a school trip this month.

7 _____ (you/work) on Friday evening?

8 _____ (I/get) a new computer for my birthday next month.

3 ⭐⭐ **Use the prompts to complete the dialogues.**

1

A: I'm in the school play.

B: Really? You/play/Romeo?
   Are you playing Romeo?

A: No/not. I/play/the Prince.
   _____

B: Who/play/Romeo?
   _____

A: Nick Parker.

2

A: you/meet/Simon this weekend?
   _____

B: Yes/I/. We/go/to the cinema.
   _____

A: he/take/you out for dinner as well?
   _____

B: No/not. He/come/to my house for dinner.
   _____

3

A: you/do/anything tomorrow?
   _____

B: No, I/not. Why?

A: I/meet/Kate at Pizza Palace.
   _____

B: So?

A: She/bring/her friend, Theresa.
   _____

B: Oh, right. Great, I'll be there.

Use your English: Make arrangements: invite, accept, refuse (with excuses)

4 ⭐ **Choose the correct options.**

1 Would you ___ to go out on Friday?

   a) want   (b) like   c) fancy

2 ___ you want to go for a picnic?

   a) Would)   b) What about   c) Do

3 Do you fancy ___ for a swim later?

   a) going   b) go   c) to go

4 I'd ___ to come.

   a) fancy   b) want   c) love

5 Thanks ___ asking.

   a) for   b) with   c) from

6 'How about having a party?' 'Yes, that ___ great.'

   a) looks   b) would   c) sounds

7 'Do you want to go out later?' 'No, I don't really ___ it, thanks.'

   a) want   b) fancy   c) like

5 ⭐⭐ **Complete the dialogues with the words and phrases from the box.**

> • What about • I can't • ~~Would you~~
> • I'm afraid • Do you • I'd love (x 2)
> • sounds great • for asking • fancy going

1 **Simon:** Hi, Matt. Hi Dave. ¹*Would you* like to come to my party on Friday?

  Matt: Sure, ² _____ to.

  Dave: Thanks ³ _____, but I don't think I can.

2 **Charles:** ⁴ _____ want to see a film tonight?

  Anna: Sorry, ⁵ _____. I'm meeting Helen.

3 **Paul:** Do you ⁶ _____ to a concert tomorrow?

  Sam: Yes, that ⁷ _____.

  Tina: ⁸ _____ I can't. We're going to my aunt's house.

4 **Lisa:** ⁹ _____ meeting in the park later?

  Donna: ¹⁰ _____ to, but I've got lots of homework.

Grammar summary

Present continuous for future arrangements

Affirmative

I**'m meeting** Tom later.
You**'re playing** at six o'clock.
He**'s coming** later.
She**'s working** this evening.
We**'re meeting** outside the theatre.
They**'re staying** for dinner.

Negative

I**'m not meeting** Tom tonight.
You **aren't playing** in this competition.
He **isn't coming** until tomorrow.
She **isn't going out** this evening.
We **aren't having** a test tomorrow.
They **aren't staying** for the night.

Questions	Short answers
Are you **meeting** Chris?	Yes, I **am**. / No, I**'m not**.
Am I **playing** today?	Yes, you **are**.
	No, you **aren't**.
Is he **flying** to Paris tomorrow?	Yes, he **is**.
	No, he **isn't**.
Is she **having** a party next week?	Yes, she **is**.
	No, she **isn't**.
Are we **getting** the bus to Gran's?	Yes, we **are**.
	No, we **aren't**.
Are they **going** anywhere tonight?	Yes, they **are**.
	No, they **aren't**.

Note

Use

- We use the present continuous for future arrangements and fixed plans.
  I'm meeting Simon.
- We often use time adverbials like *next week, at the weekend, later* to show that the activity is in the future.
  I'm going to my aunt's this weekend.

Form

- We use the correct form of the verb *to be + verb + ing*. The form is exactly the same as the present continuous for things happening now.

Common mistakes

- We can't use the present continuous to make future predictions.
  It's raining soon. ✗
  It's going to rain soon. ✓

1c They're the best films ever!

Vocabulary: Adjectives of opinion

1 ⭐ **Choose the correct options.**

1 I didn't really understand the film because it was very ___.
   a) violent   b) confusing

2 What a great horror film. It was really ___!
   a) scary   b) funny

3 I can't believe this film is for twelve-year-olds. It's much too ___.
   a) violent   b) sad

4 It was really ___. I couldn't stop laughing.
   a) complicated   b) funny

5 It was so ___ when the hero died. I cried and cried.
   a) confusing   b) sad

6 It was a good horror film and the music made it even more ___.
   a) frightening   b) violent

7 You have to watch very carefully because it's quite a ___ story.
   a) scary   b) complicated

2 ⭐⭐ **Complete the adjectives.**

The film was very good.

It was …

1 a m a z i n g
2 _ w _ s _ _ _
3 _ x _ _ l _ _ n _
4 _ x _ _ t _ _ _
5 _ _ j _ y _ _ _ e
6 _ _ t _ _ _ s _ _ _ g

The film was very bad.

It was …

7 _ w _ u _
8 _ o _ _ _ g
9 _ _ s _ p _ _ _ _ t _ _ _
10 _ u _ l

Grammar: Comparison of adjectives
much + comparative adjective *(not) as*
… as; Superlatives

3 ⭐ **Complete the sentences with the words from the box.**

> • sad • more • isn't • worse • as • ~~than~~
> • much • the • worst

1 Can we watch the film on Channel 2? It's better *than* this one.

2 What a terrible film. It was _____ than doing my homework!

3 Mum. Can I watch *The Ring*? It isn't _____ scary as *The Grudge*!

4 The _____ film I saw on television last year was *The Avengers*.

5 European films are _____ interesting than American ones.

6 I think Daniel Day Lewis is _____ best actor in the world.

7 The film wasn't as _____ as I was expecting.

8 Jim Carrey is funny, but he _____ as funny as Ben Stiller.

9 I think films now are _____ more scary than when we were young.

4 ⭐⭐ **Complete text with the correct form of the adjectives in brackets. Add any other words necessary.**

James Bond films are now more than fifty years old. But which one is [1]*the best* (good) and who is your favourite Bond? Here's what we found out.

[2]_____ (good) Bond is Sean Connery but [3]_____ (exciting) film is *Skyfall*. Sean Connery's best film was *Goldfinger*, but it isn't [4]_____ (good) as any of the Daniel Craig films. [5]_____ (scary) baddie was Baron Samedi in *Live and Let Die*.

The new Bond films are [6]_____ (exciting) the old films. That's what most young people think. They say that the old films were

7_____ (dull) the new ones but older

people don't think the new films are 8_____

(enjoyable) as the old ones.

What about Bond songs? Some of you said that

Adele's *Skyfall* was amazing but others say it

was 9_____ (dull) of all the Bond songs.

Your favourite Bond singer is Shirley Bassey. She

sang two songs and you said that *Goldfinger* was

10_____ (good) *Diamonds Are Forever*.

5 ★★★ **Use the prompts and the information in the table to write sentences.**

Old or New?

Star Wars	Exciting	Enjoyable
Old	★★★	★★★★★
New	★★★★	★★★

1 The old Star Wars films/not/exciting/new Star Wars films

The old Star Wars films aren't as exciting as the new Star Wars films.

2 The old Star Wars films/much/enjoyable/new

_____

3 good/film/is/the first one

_____

4 bad/film/is/the fifth one

_____

Ocean's Eleven	Acting	How cool is it?
Old	★★	★★★★
New	★★★	★★★★

5 The acting in the old film/not/good/the acting in the new film

_____

6 The actors in the original film/cool/the actors in the new film

_____

7 They not/good-looking/George Clooney and Brad Pitt though!

_____

Grammar summary

Comparison of adjectives
Comparatives and superlatives
Regular short adjectives
New York is **(much) bigger** than London. DVD's are (aren't) **as good as** films in the cinema. *Slender Man* is **the scariest** game on the internet.
Regular long adjectives
Horror films are **more frightening** than computer games. Normal films are (aren't) **as enjoyable as** 3D films. My brother is **the most annoying** person I know.
Irregular adjectives
Skyfall is **(much) better** than *Casino Royale*. Anne Hathaway is **the best young** actress in Hollywood. The film is **(much) worse** than the book. Surfing the Net is **the worst** way to spend the evening.

Note

Use

- We use comparatives + *than* to compare two things. *Matt Damon is younger than Robert De Niro.*
- We use *as* + adjective + *as* to say that two things are the same and *not as* + adjective + *as* to say that two things are different. *Playing football is (not) as enjoyable as playing tennis.*
- We use superlatives to compare more than two people or things. *I'm the tallest girl in my class.*

Spelling rules

After one syllable adjectives:

- We usually add -*er*/-*est*. *young – younger/youngest*
- After -*e*, we add -*r*/-*st* *nice – nicer/nicest*
- After one vowel and one consonant, we double the final consonant and add -*er*/-*est*. *big – bigger/biggest*

For two or more syllable adjectives:

- We usually use *more*/*most* + adjective. *interesting – more/most interesting*
- After two syllable adjectives ending in -*y*, we change the -*y* to -*i* and add -*er*/-*est*. *pretty – prettier/prettiest*

Common mistakes

~~Sue isn't so nice like Jane.~~ ✗

Sue isn't as nice as Jane. ✓

~~Beth is more older than Mandy.~~ ✗

Beth is older than Mandy. ✓

1 Put the words in the box into the correct spaces.

> • ~~cello~~ • violin • awesome • techno • dull
> • awful • clarinet • enjoyable • classical
> • flute • jazz

What instrument did you play?

1 _cello_ _____ _____ _____

What kind of music did they play?

2 _____ _____ _____

What did you think of the concert? (It was great.)

3 _____ _____

What do you think of the CD? (It's bad.)

4 _____ _____

.../10

2 Use the prompts to write questions and answers.

1 A: you/want/come/to a concert tonight?

   B: Yes/I/come

   A: Do you want to come to a concert tonight?

   B: Yes, I'll come.

2 A: When/you/do/your homework?

   B: Er./I/do/it after this film, I promise.

   _____

   _____

3 A: When/you/meet/Amy?

   B: I/meet/her tomorrow at eleven o'clock

   _____

   _____

4 A: you/fancy/go/to the cinema tonight?

   B: I/can't. We/go/to my grandmother's tonight

   _____

   _____

5 A: you/like/come/to my party on Saturday?

   B: afraid/can't but/thanks/ask

   _____

   _____

6 A: you/still/live here in ten years' time?

   B: No/not. It's boring here.

   _____

   _____

.../10

3 Complete the dialogue with the correct form of the words in brackets.

A: The [1]_best_ (good) thing about *Life of Pi* was the 3D effects. They were [2]_____ (good) than in *Avatar*.

B: No way. They weren't as [3]_____ (good) as *Avatar*. That was brilliant.

A: Do you want to see *Avatar 2*?

B: No. Second films are always [4]_____ (bad) than originals.

A: Not always. *Madagascar 2* was [5]_____ (funny) than *Madagascar 1* and *Pirates of the Caribbean 2* was [6]_____ (enjoyable) than the first film.

B: You're joking! *Pirates of the Caribbean 2* was the [7]_____ (complicated) film ever and it was the [8]_____ (bad) of the four films.

A: Yeah, it wasn't as [9]_____ (interesting) as the other films but Penelope Cruz is the [10]_____ (beautiful) actress in Hollywood.

B: And the [11]_____ (scary)!

.../10

4 Complete the second sentence so that it has the same meaning as the first.

1 Stephen isn't as old as me.

   Stephen is _younger than_ me.

2 My plan is to get a summer job this year.

   I'm _____ this year.

3 I've arranged to visit my cousin on Friday.

   I'm _____ on Friday.

4 No actor is better than Robert De Niro!

   Robert De Niro _____ in the world!

5 Rap isn't better than techno and it isn't worse.

   Rap is _____ techno.

6 French is difficult, but German is very difficult.

   German is _____ French.

.../10

🎧 **LISTEN AND CHECK YOUR SCORE**

Total	.../40

.../10

1 Skills practice

SKILLS FOCUS: READING AND WRITING

Read

1 **Read about a music festival and match the headings (1–3) to the paragraphs (A–C).**

1 Lots of things to do

2 See your work at the festival

3 See interesting and famous people

 SOUNDTRACK FESTIVAL

| Home | News | Music | About | Sign up |

A 1
The Soundtrack Festival started in 2008. I read about it on the internet and decided to go. It was brilliant. As well as watching films, I listened to film makers talking about their work, watched musicians and bands in concert and learned how to turn a book into a film.

B ___
I went to the festival a few years ago. There were a lot of interesting people there. I know it doesn't attract Oscar winning actors or directors but I didn't mind that. When I was there, I saw the rock band Gong, composers, film producers, poets and the musician, John Cale.

C ___
I really enjoyed watching films by unknown film makers. Some of them were full-length movies and others were short films. They were as good as the films they showed made by more famous film makers. Anyone can send a film to the festival and they show the best. It's completely free. I'm going to try next year.

2 **Read the text again and answer true (T), false (F) or doesn't say (DS).**

1 At the festival, you can listen to music.   *T*

2 At the festival, you can meet Oscar winning actors.   ___

3 'Gong' is the title of a film.   ___

4 The full-length films were better than the short films.   ___

5 The festival doesn't show all the films people send to it.   ___

Write

3 **Complete the email with the words from the box.**

- Hi • going • Bye • How's • Do (x 2)
- now • fancy • want

¹<u>Hi</u> Rebecca,

² _____ it ³ _____? I hope you enjoyed the concert last night.
I'm meeting Ben and Josh at Burger City this afternoon. We're meeting at three o'clock. I know the food isn't great, but it's cheaper than other places. ⁴ _____ you ⁵ _____ meeting us there?
After lunch, I'm going to go shopping. I need to buy some new shoes. ⁶ _____ you ⁷ _____ to come with me? You're always good at choosing clothes.
I hope you can come. It'll be lovely to see you and you can tell me all about the concert.
⁸ _____ for ⁹ _____.

Vicky

4 **Use the notes to write a reply to Vicky.**

- Greeting: Thank Vicky for the email. Tell her your opinion of the concert.

- Main message: Tell Vicky you can't meet for lunch – your aunt is coming for dinner – you would like to meet later and go shopping – you need to buy clothes, too.

- Details and arrangements: Arrange when and where to meet. Suggest something to do after shopping.

- Summary and conclusion: Thank Vicky again. Tell her you hope she has a nice lunch.

Vocabulary: Household jobs

1 ★ **Complete the puzzle.**

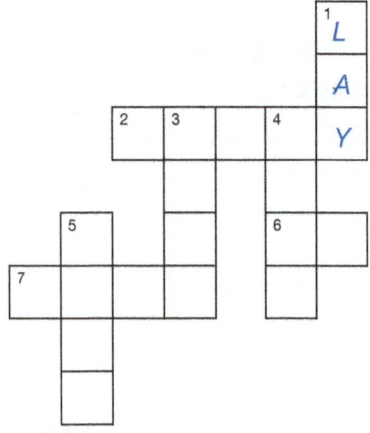

1 *lay* the table

2 _____ the dishwasher

3 _____ the breakfast

4 _____ your room

5 _____ the car

6 _____ the cleaning

7 _____ the rubbish out

2 ★ **Look at the pictures and complete the jobs.**

1

do the *vacuuming*

2

_____ the _____

3

_____ the _____

4

_____ the _____

5

_____ the _____

6

_____ the _____

7

_____ the _____

Grammar: Present perfect simple with time adverbials *ever, never, already, just, yet*

3 ★ **Choose the correct responses.**

1 You look tired.

  a) Yes, I've already tidied my room.

  b) Yes, I've just tidied my room.

2 Do your homework!

  a) I haven't done it yet.

  b) I've already done it.

3 Have you ever lost something important?

  a) No, never.   b) No, not yet.

4 Your hair looks different today.

  a) Yes, I've had it cut.

  b) Yes, I've already had it cut.

5 Have you done the washing-up yet?

  a) No, I've already walked in the door.

  b) No, I've just walked in the door.

6 Why don't you want to see the film?

  a) I've already seen it. b) I've never seen it.

4 ★★ **Use the prompts to write questions and answers.**

1 A: you/ever/see/the Eiffel Tower?

  B: ✓. I/be/to the top twice.

  A: Have you ever seen the Eiffel Tower?

  B: Yes, I have. I've been to the top twice.

2 A: you/tidy/your room yet?

  B: I/start/but/I not finish/yet

  _____

  _____

3 A: you/ever/find/money in the street?

  B: ✗. but I/lose/lots of money!

  _____

  _____

4 A: Jack/do/the washing-up yet?

  B: ✓. and/he/already/empty/the

  dishwasher

  _____

  _____

5 ⭐⭐⭐⭐ **Complete the dialogues with the prompts from the box.**

> • Yes, just/buy • I/never/be/there • I/never/make • ~~No/already/see~~ • No, not/finish/yet

1

A: Do you want to watch this DVD?

B: *No, I've already seen it.*

2

A: Can I borrow this book?

B: _____

3

A: Is that shirt new?

B: _____

4

A: Do you like New York?

B: _____

5

A: So, how do we make a cake?

B: I don't know. _____

Grammar summary

Present perfect simple with time adverbials *ever, never, already, just, yet*
Present perfect simple with *just* and *already*
I've just finished my homework.
He**'s already gone** out.
Present perfect simple with *yet*
Have they **arrived yet**?
She **hasn't woken up yet**.
Present perfect simple with *ever* and *never*
Have you **ever been** to Venice?
Has he **ever forgotten** your birthday?
We**'ve never been** late to school.
She**'s never eaten** Chinese food.

Note

Use

- We use the present perfect simple with *just* to say that something happened a very short time ago.
  I'm tired because I've just woken up.
- We use *already* to emphasise that something has happened before now.
  We've already done this exercise!
- We use *yet* in negative sentences and questions to mean *up to now*.
  I haven't done the washing-up yet (but I will do it).
  Have you tidied your room yet?
- We use *never* to mean *at no time in my life*.
  I have never failed an exam.
- We use *ever* in questions to mean *at any time in your life*.
  Have you ever had a summer job?

Form

- We put *just, already, ever* and *never* before the main verb.
  *I have **never cooked** dinner.*
  *We have **just finished** our exam.*
  *They have **already left**.*
  *Have you **ever seen** a famous person?*
- We put *yet* at the end of negative sentences and questions.
  *Have you finished **yet**?*
  *He hasn't sent me an email **yet**.*

Common mistakes

~~I haven't never been to Rome.~~ ✗

I've never been to Rome. ✓

~~Have you done your homework already?~~ ✗

Have you done your homework yet? ✓

2b He asked me out.

Vocabulary: Relationship words and phrases

1 ⭐ **Complete the sentences with one word in each space.**

1 I'm really annoyed _with_ my brother. He's taken my MP3 player without asking.

2 I had an argument _____ Tom and now I'm really upset.

3 Hi, you're new here, aren't you? Do you want to _____ friends with us?

4 Julie started going _____ with Chris when they were in Year 11.

5 Did you fall _____ with Luke because he forgot your birthday?

6 I get _____ well with most of the people in my class.

7 My friend's parents are going to _____ divorced and she's really sad.

8 Peter asked me _____ on a date. Do you think I should say 'Yes'?

9 I was really angry with Rob, but he said sorry and now we've made _____.

2 ⭐⭐ **Look at the pictures and complete the phrases with one word in each space.**

1 John and Emily met at a party and immediately f_ell_ in l_ove_ w_ith_ each other.

2 Emily b_____ u_____ w_____ John after an argument, but they soon got back together.

3 John g_____ e_____ t_____ Emily in a restaurant when they were both twenty-two years old.

2 John g_____ m_____ t_____ Emily in 2012.

Grammar: Present perfect simple and past simple; Time adverbials

3 ⭐⭐ **Complete the sentences with one of the verbs in brackets in the past simple and the other in the present perfect.**

1 I _met_ (meet) Eric three weeks ago. My parents _have just met_ (just meet) Eric.

2 I _____ (do) my homework last night.
I _____ (already do) my homework.

3 I _____ (never be) in a school play.
I _____ (not be) in the school play last year.

4 _____ (you ever go) to Greece?
_____ (you go) to Greece last summer?

4 ⭐⭐⭐ **Use the prompts to write questions and sentences.**

1 A: you/do/the washing-up yet?
B: ✓. I/do/it this morning.
A: Have you done the washing-up yet?
B: Yes, I have. I did it this morning.

2 A: When you/go to ask/Melanie/out?
B: I/already/ask/her. I/ask/her yesterday.
A: _____
B: _____

3 A: you/ever/be/in love?
B: ✓. I/fall/in love last night.
A: _____
B: _____

4 A: I/never/have/an argument with my sister.
B: Yes, you have. You/have/one last week
A: _____
B: _____

Use your English: Talk about problems: suggestions and advice

5 ⬛⭐ **Complete the sentences with one word in each space.**

1 I don't k_now_ what to do about my annoying brother.

2 I'm a b_____ worried about my schoolwork.

3 What's the m_____?

4 M_____ you should eat less junk food.

5 W_____ don't you ask your parents for advice?

6 You look f_____ u_____.

7 I don't think you s_____ break up with her.

8 You look w_____.

6 ⬛⭐⭐ **Complete the dialogue with the phrases from the box.**

- why don't you   • I'm a bit worried about
- Maybe you should   • What's up?
- I don't think you should
- ~~You look a bit miserable~~
- I don't know what to do

A: Hello, Seth. ¹_You look a bit miserable_.

² _____

B: ³ _____ my relationship with Rachael. We had an argument yesterday and she broke up with me.

⁴ _____ about it.

A: I see. Well, ⁵ _____ phone her and apologise?

B: I tried that but she refused to talk to me.

A: ⁶ _____ send her some flowers first.

B: I haven't got any money for flowers. I think I'll go round to her house and bang on her front door until she agrees to talk to me.

A: ⁷ _____ do that. Her parents won't be very happy and she'll be even angrier with you. I'll lend you some money for flowers.

Grammar summary

Present perfect simple and past simple
Present perfect simple
I**'ve already eaten** dinner.
She**'s never been** late before.
Have you **asked** her out **yet**?
Past simple
I **ate** dinner **half an hour ago**.
She **wasn't** late **yesterday**.
Did you **ask** her out **last weekend**?

Note

Use

- We use the present perfect simple when the time period is unfinished or with certain time adverbials such as _just, yet_ or _already_, which show a connection with the present.
  Have you ever been to America? (in your life)
  I've never been in love. (in my life)
- We use the past simple when the time period is finished.
  I went to the cinema yesterday.
  What did you do last weekend?

Common problems

- We can use some time expressions with both the present perfect simple and the past simple.
  Have you seen Ben this morning? (It is still morning.)
  Did you see Ben this morning? (It is now later in the day.)

Common mistakes

~~Did you ever fall in love?~~ ✗
Have you ever fallen in love? ✓

2c People who you can trust.

Vocabulary: Family

1 ⭐ **Look at the family tree and answer the questions.**

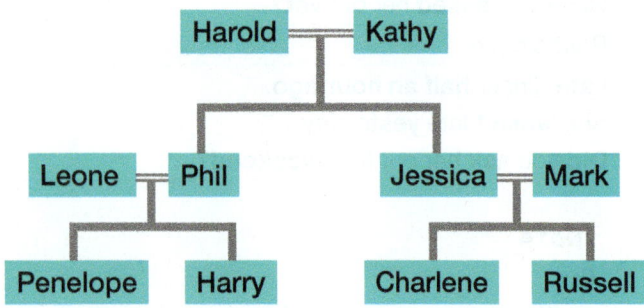

1 Who is Phil's wife?   *Leone*
2 Who is Harry's aunt?   _____
3 Who are Penelope's grandparents?   _____
4 Who are Harry's cousins?   _____
5 Who is Kathy's son?   _____
6 Who is Russell's uncle?   _____
7 Who is Mark's daughter?   _____
8 Who is Phil's niece?   _____
9 Who is Jessica's brother?   _____
10 Who is Jessica's nephew?   _____

2 ⭐⭐ **Complete the sentences with the words from the box. There are three extra words.**

> • mother-in-law • sister-in-law
> • stepmother • stepfather • stepsister
> • single • fiancé • fiancée • married

1 Your wife's mother is your *mother-in-law*.
2 A person who doesn't have a husband or wife is _____.
3 The woman who married your father when he divorced your mum is your _____.
4 The boy you are engaged to is your _____.
5 Your husband's sister is your _____.
6 The girl you are engaged to is your _____.

Grammar: Defining relative clauses with *who, which, that, whose, where*

3 ⭐ **Complete the sentences with the relative pronouns from the box.**

> • who (x 2) • which • where (x 2) • whose

1 I've got a cousin <u>who</u> plays football for Arsenal Under 16s.
2 This is the restaurant _____ my boyfriend proposed to me.
3 My sister is married to a man _____ parents live in a castle.
4 This is the school _____ I want to go to.
5 I know a shop _____ you can work this summer.
6 The couple _____ were getting married didn't look very happy.

4 ⭐⭐ **Choose the option which is NOT possible.**

1 My girlfriend is someone …
  a) I love very much.   b) me very much.
  c) my parents get on with very well.
2 This is the church where …
  a) my parents got married in.
  b) a lot of local people get married.
  c) they filmed *Four Weddings and a Funeral*.
3 I want to meet someone whose …
  a) got a lot of money.   b) parents are rich.
  c) ideas about life are the same as mine.
4 The wedding …
  a) I remember best was my cousin's.
  b) we read about cost £10,000.
  c) took place here last week was between a prince and an actress.
5 I've met someone that …
  a) I love very much.   b) I care about him a lot.
  c) is never late.

5 ★★ **Complete the sentences with who, which, where or whose. Put the pronoun in brackets if it can be omitted.**

1 She's a girl <u>who</u> makes me smile every time I see her.

2 She's a girl <u>(who)</u> I can tell my secrets to.

3 That was a day _____ I will never forget.

4 That was the day _____ changed my life.

5 She's the girl _____ brother is a famous singer.

6 We went to a café _____ I never want to go back to again!

7 We went to a café _____ a sandwich cost £8!

6 ★★★ **Join the sentences with relative pronouns. Make any other changes necessary.**

1 She's a woman. Her husband was a famous footballer.

<u>She's a woman whose husband was a famous footballer.</u>

2 She's a woman. She was in a pop group.

_____

3 It's an art gallery. You can see the Mona Lisa there.

_____
_____

4 It's an art gallery. Lots of people visit it each year.

_____

5 He's an actor. He's won the Best Actor Oscar three times.

_____
_____

6 He's an actor. His father was a famous poet.

_____

7 It's a place. It's a district of Los Angeles.

_____
_____

8 It's a place. Lots of films are made there.

_____

Grammar summary

Defining relative clauses with who, which, that, whose, where

People (who/that)
I know a boy **who** was on television.
These are the people (**who/that**) I told you about.

Things (which/that)
My girlfriend said some things **which/that** annoyed me.
This is the shop (**which/that**) I buy most of my clothes from.

Possessions (whose)
Mr Clarke is the teacher **whose** tests are the most difficult.

Places (where)
This is the town **where** I grew up.

Note

Use

- We use defining relative clauses to give essential information about the person, place or thing we are talking about.
  That's the book which I was telling you about.

- In conversation and informal language, we often replace *who* or *which* with *that*.
  Is this the shop that refused to give you your money back?
  She's the girl that smiled at me.

Form

- We can omit *who, which* or *that* when they refer to the object of the sentence.
  That's the CD (which/that) I want to buy.
  She's the girl (who/that) I love.

- We can't miss out *where* or *whose*.

Common mistakes

~~This is the classroom where have exams in.~~ ✗
This is the classroom where we have exams. ✓
This is the classroom (which/that) we have exams in. ✓
~~This is the boy which I met at the disco.~~ ✗
This is the boy (who/that) I met at the disco. ✓

1 Complete the text with one word in each space.

Hi Marcin,

Thanks for your email. This is a photo of my family. My mum and dad [1]*got* divorced three years [2]_____. She's going to [3]_____ married to the man in the photo next year so I'll have a [4]_____. He's got a son, Simon, so I'll have a [5]_____, too. The other woman is my mum's sister, my [6]_____. She hasn't got any children so I haven't got any [7]_____.
I hope I get [8]_____ well with Simon. At least there will be someone else to help with the jobs in the house. I [9]_____ the cooking every day. Of course, I [10]_____ my bed in the morning and I [11]_____ my room every Saturday. After that, I'm free to go out. I usually go out with my friend Samantha but last week, she [12]_____ in love with a boy at a party. He asked her [13]_____ on Saturday but they may break [14]_____ before then. Samantha doesn't stay with boys for very long! She always [15]_____ an argument about something!
Write soon.

Lucy

.../14

2 Choose the correct options.

1 I've been to Italy twice but I've ___ seen Rome.

  a) ever   b) yet   c) never

2 Have you emptied the dishwasher ___?

  a) already   b) ever   c) yet

3 Did you enjoy the film ___?

  a) yesterday b) already c) yet

4 Have you seen Joe ___?

  a) yesterday b) recently c) last night

5 How much work have you done ___?

  a) so far   b) on Saturday c) at the weekend

6 Where ___ you go yesterday?

  a) were   b) did   c) have

7 When ___ this photo?

  a) do you take b) have you taken

  c) did you take

.../6

3 Complete the dialogue with the words from the box.

> • whose • went • yet • who • just
> • which • ~~Did~~ • has • out • ago • Have

Meg: [1]*Did* you see Jake last night? [2]_____ you made up with him [3]_____?

Jo: Yes, and we promised not to fall [4]_____ again. There's a concert [5]_____ his brother's band are going to play in on Saturday.

Meg: Saturday? We arranged to go to the cinema a long time [6]_____.

Jo: I know but there will be someone at the concert [7]_____ I think you'll want to meet. Tom Stephens. The boy [8]_____ family moved to France when we were in Year 9. You were heartbroken! He's [9]_____ come back. You [10]_____ out with him, didn't you?

Meg: No, but I wanted to. OK, I'll be there. I wonder if he [11]_____ changed much.

.../10

4 Cross out the two incorrect words in each sentence and write the correct ones.

1 My cousin ~~is~~ just ~~gone~~ engaged. *has, got*

2 I get up very well with my cousin and I'm very close with her mum. _____

3 My parents haven't met Neil already, but they have saw his photo. _____

4 I fell on love with a boy what I met at a party. _____

5 You've never made the washing-up and you've never done your bed. _____

6 I find it easy to get friends with people I meet, but I often do arguments with my brother. _____

.../10

🎧 **LISTEN AND CHECK YOUR SCORE**

Total	.../40

2 Skills practice

SKILLS FOCUS: READING, LISTENING AND WRITING

Read

1 **Read the text and choose the best title.**

A Max's big argument

B Max's mum makes a decision

C Max wants more freedom

Max was tired. He was always tired. His school books were open, but he couldn't concentrate. At that moment, his father walked into the room.

'Have you finished, your homework yet?' he said.

Max shouted, 'No, I haven't and I won't finish it if you keep coming in.'

His father gently said: 'You've done enough. Go to bed.'

This time, Max didn't argue and, he was soon asleep.

Downstairs, his mum was worried. 'He's so tired. He'll be ill,' she said.

The next day, Max apologised to his dad. 'I just don't know what to do. I've got lots of homework, Sylvia always wants to go out and I have to go to football practice, too.'

'You have to decide what's most important,' said his father.

Max knew he was right. He knew he was lucky that his parents didn't tell him what to do. 'But you can't go out with Sylvia from Sunday to Thursday,' said his mother, suddenly. His father looked at her in surprise. Max was shocked. 'But mum,' he said 'that's not fair.' But he was happy that his mum had decided for him!

2 **Read the text again and answer true (T) or false (F).**

1 At the start of the story, Max is working hard. _T_

2 Max's father tells Max what to do. ＿＿

3 Max's parents are both worried about his

health. ＿＿

4 Max's problem is that he hasn't got enough

time to do everything. ＿＿

5 The person who makes Max's life easier in the

end is his dad. ＿＿

Listen

3 🎧 **Listen to the conversation and decide who the two people are.**

a) A boyfriend and girlfriend who have broken up.

b) A boyfriend and girlfriend.

c) A boy and a girl who are friends.

4 🎧 **Listen again and answer the questions.**

1 When is Shelly's party?

Wednesday

2 Who did Kevin Gates go out with in the past?

_____.

3 How did Kevin feel when they broke up?

_____.

4 What does Liz want Max to do?

_____.

5 When is Max going to talk to Sylvia?

_____.

Write

5 **Complete the invitation with the words and phrases from the box.**

- What about going • See you tomorrow
- It will be • are coming • H̶i̶ • tell me
- I'm not having • I'll ask • Do you want

[1]_Hi_ Steve,

It's my birthday on Thursday. I hate having a birthday on a school day! [2]_____ a normal day with an early start and homework! Friday will be a bit more exciting. My aunt and uncle and my two cousins [3]_____ to our house for a small family party.

[4]_____ a party for friends this year, but I'd like to do something. [5]_____ to go to the cinema with me on Saturday? There's a good action film on at four o'clock in the afternoon.

[6]_____ into town early and having a pizza or something for lunch first? I think [7]_____ Heather and Sally, too.

Think about it and [8]_____ at school tomorrow.

[9]_____.

Max.

3a Too big to see it all on foot.

Grammar: *too* + adjective/adverb + *to; (not)* + adjective/adverb + *enough to*

1 ⭐ **Complete the sentences with one word in each space.**

1 I wrote carefully, but I didn't write carefully *enough*.

2 I swam well, but I didn't swim well enough _____ win.

3 I worked hard, but I didn't work _____ enough to pass my exam.

4 I wrote my test _____ quickly and made lots of mistakes.

5 I spoke quietly, but I didn't speak quietly _____ and my teacher heard me.

2 ⭐⭐ **Use the prompts to write sentences.**

Where do you want to go for your winter holiday?

1 Moscow?

It/cold *It's too cold.*

2 Jamaica?

a) It/far _____.

b) I/not rich _____.

3 Skiing?

a) I/scared _____.

b) It/dangerous _____.

4 Rome?

a) It/rainy _____.

b) My Italian/not good

_____.

5 London

a) It/big _____.

b) The food/not tasty

_____.

3 ⭐⭐⭐ **Complete the second sentence so that it has the same meaning as the first. Use the word in capitals.**

1 I'm too young to go on holiday with my friends. ENOUGH

I'm *not old enough to go on holiday with my friends*.

2 My PC is too slow for this game. FAST

My PC _____.

3 I was too slow to win the race. RAN

I _____.

4 I'm not tall enough to play for the school basketball team. SHORT

I'm _____.

5 I'm not good enough at French to understand this book. SPEAK

I don't _____.

6 We can't go out for a meal because all the restaurants are shut. LATE

It's _____.

Vocabulary: Adjectives and nouns of measurement

4 ⭐ **Complete the text with one word in each space.**

The London Eye is great. It's quite [1]e*xpensive*. Tickets cost about £20 each for adults, but it's worth it. The Eye is 135 metres [2]h_____ so you get a great view from the top. There are thirty-two glass rooms that you stand in for your journey. They are very [3]b_____. Twenty-five people can go in each one and there is still lots of room to move around. The Eye isn't very [4]f_____. It's slow enough for people to get on and off easily.
It isn't very [5]o_____, but I can't imagine London without it. Big Ben isn't very [6]f_____ from The Eye and it's a nice walk. You just cross the River Thames, which is about 200 metres [7]w_____, on Westminster Bridge, which is about 250 metres [8]l_____.

3 CITY LIFE

Vocabulary: Transport

5 ⭐ **Match the definitions (1–9) to the words (a–i).**

1 You cycle on this.   _e_

2 It's like a small motorbike.   ___

3 You fly in this.   ___

4 You can phone for one to take you
   where you want to go.   ___

5 It's like a train but below the city.   ___

6 It's like a big car (or a small lorry).   ___

7 You can catch this at a railway station.   ___

8 It travels on water.   ___

9 You drive it.   ___

a) underground   f) van
b) train   g) car
c) moped   h) helicopter
d) boat   i) taxi
e) bike

6 ⭐⭐ **Look at the pictures and complete the puzzle.**

```
¹S C O O T E R
    ²  R
  ³    A
  ⁴    N
       ⁵S
       ⁶P
     ⁷  O
  ⁸    R
       ⁹T
```

Grammar summary

too + adjective/adverb + *to*
You're **too young to** buy fireworks.
She types **too slowly to** be a secretary.

(not) + adjective/adverb + *enough to*
You're **clever enough to** get into university.
She **runs fast** enough to be a sports star.
He is**n't strong enough to** lift his bags.
He does**n't sing well enough** to win the competition.

Note

Use

- We use *too* + adjective/adverb + *to* and *(not)* + adjective/adverb + *enough* + *to* to say that something is not possible.
  He's too young to play with us. (It's impossible for him to play with us because of his age.)
  She speaks too quietly to be an actress. (It's impossible for her to be an actress because of the quietness of her voice.)

- We use adjective/adverb + *enough* + *to* to say something is possible.
  She's good enough to win this competition. (It is possible for her to win this competition.)

- We don't use *too* or *enough* with adjectives which don't have comparative or superlative forms, e.g. *impossible, dead, English* – things can't be more or less impossible, dead or English.

Common mistakes

~~He is enough old to understand the rules.~~ ✗
He is old enough to understand the rules. ✓
~~He's too unfit for being a footballer.~~ ✗
He's too unfit to be a footballer. ✓

3b You can't miss it.

Vocabulary: Places in town

1 ⭐ **Match the beginnings (1–10) to the endings (a–g) to make places in town. Some beginnings match the same ending.**

1 swimming	a) centre
2 petrol	b) gallery
3 police	c) pool
4 sports	d) station
5 town	e) shop
6 tourist information	f) office
7 music	g) hall
8 art	
9 post	
10 shopping	

2 ⭐⭐ **Complete the places.**

1 My mum works here. She sells coffee and cakes.   c*afé*

2 Mr Smith works here. People go to him to ask for money or give him their money.
   b_____

3 Three hundred people work here. They make cars.   f_____

4 Miss Jenkins, the nurse, and Miss Taylor, the doctor, work here.   h_____

5 We get our daily newspaper from here.
   n_____

6 My friend worked here with ten other people. They all had a desk and a computer. My friend hated it.   o_____

7 You can book your holiday on the internet or you can go here.   t_____ a_____

8 When I want a book to read, I go here.
   l_____

9 You can get a holiday job as a waiter here.
   r_____

10 It's a great place to buy food. It's cheaper than smaller shops.   s_____

3 ⭐⭐ **Complete the description with one letter in each space.**

Our town is very beautiful. In the centre of the town is a lovely ¹*square* with cafés and beautiful old buildings. There's an interesting ²_ _ s _ u _ where you can find out about the town's history. Not far from the centre, there is a big ³_ _ r _ with trees and grass. It's a great place to walk on a sunny day and there's a small ⁴_ o _ with animals like wolves and deer in it. There aren't any elephants or lions, though. There's a ⁵_ h _ _ t _ _ where you can see great plays. There are two ⁶_ _ t _ _ s where you can stay the night. One is big and expensive, but the smaller one is nicer. Oh, and in Station Road, just past the ⁷_ h _ _ m _ c _, is my ⁸_ c _ _ _ l.

Phrases

4 ⭐⭐ **Choose the correct options.**

Mike:	Excuse me.
Tracey:	Yes?
Mike:	I'm a bit ¹**far** / **lost** / **wrong**. I'm trying to get to the café.
Tracey:	The café?
Mike:	Oh, I ²**think** / **mean** / **suppose** there are lots of cafés.
Tracey:	Yes, there are. Tell me about the one you want.
Mike:	Eh?
Tracey:	I ³**guess** / **suppose** / **mean** what it looks like, what kind of food it sells.
Mike:	Oh. It's French. It's got very good cakes.
Tracey:	Oh, I know. 'Le Soleil'. Come with me.
Mike:	Thanks … is it far … through the park? Wow, it's a long way … Ah, at last, the town centre. What ⁴**more** / **now** / **for**?
Tracey:	We just cross the road and it's over there. Look.
Mike:	Oh great. Thanks. Can I buy you a cake?
Tracey:	Mmm, I'd love one.

Use your English: Ask for and give directions

5 ⭐ **Match the pictures to the directions from the box.**

- Go straight on. • ~~Turn right~~.
- Cross the road. • Take the first on the right.
- Turn left. • The bank is next to the station.
- Go past the bank. • Take the second on the left.
- The bank is opposite the station.
- Go right out of the station.

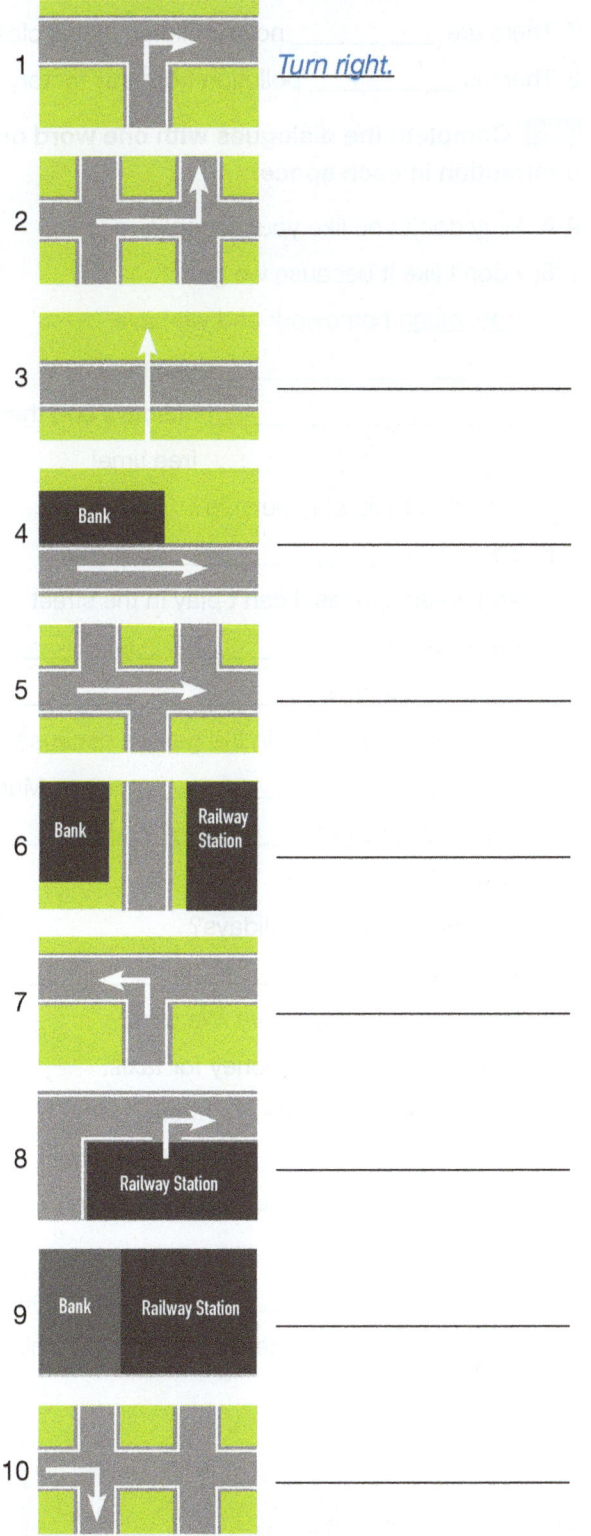

1 _Turn right._

2 _____

3 _____

4 _____

5 _____

6 _____

7 _____

8 _____

9 _____

10 _____

6 ⭐⭐ **Complete the dialogues with one word in each space.**

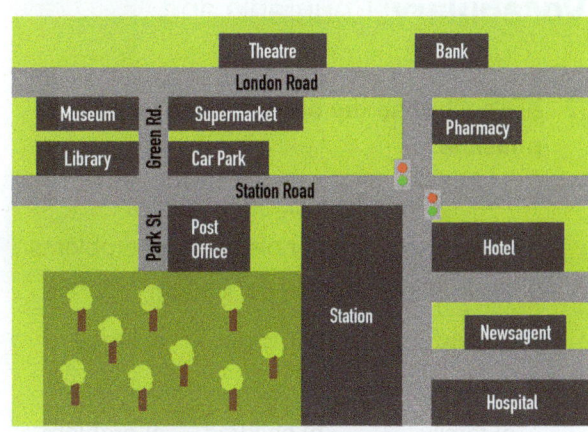

1 **A:** Excuse me. How can I get to the theatre?

 B: Go ¹_right_ out of the station and ²_____ the first turning on your ³_____. Go ⁴_____ the pharmacy and turn ⁵_____. The theatre is ⁶_____ the supermarket.

2 **A:** How can I get to the museum from the hospital?

 B: Go left ⁷_____ of the hospital and turn ⁸_____ at the corner. Take the ⁹_____ turning on your left and go straight on. At the corner, turn right and the museum is on the left ¹⁰_____ to the library.

7 ⭐⭐⭐ **Complete the dialogues with one word in each space.**

1 **A:** ¹_Excuse_ me. Can you tell me the ²_____ to the post office, please?

 B: Yes, of course. Go ³_____ on along this road for about 200 metres. Go ⁴_____ the supermarket and then ⁵_____ the road at the traffic lights. You'll see the post office ⁶_____ your right.

2 **A:** Sorry to ⁷_____ you, but ⁸_____ do I get to the sports centre?

 B: Go left ⁹_____ of here. ¹⁰_____ the third turning on your left. That's Chapel Street. The sports centre is next ¹¹_____ an Italian restaurant.

 A: Thank you.

 B: You're ¹²_____.

3c We throw away too many things.

Vocabulary: Countable and uncountable nouns

1 ⭐ **Choose the option which is NOT possible.**

1 There are a lot of ___.
   a) rubbish   b) holes   c) problems

2 There is some ___ in the kitchen.
   a) food   b) things   c) luggage

3 I've got a big ___.
   a) family   b) children   c) problem

4 We need more ___.
   a) informations   b) news   c) schools

5 We've got a problem with ___.
   a) pollution   b) traffic   c) factory

6 There aren't many ___.
   a) money   b) gardens   c) streets

2 ⭐⭐ **Tick (✓) the sentences which are correct. Put a cross (✗) after the sentences which are incorrect.**

1 I haven't got a food. ✗
2 There isn't any food. ✓
3 How many children are there?
4 My sister's got a child.
5 How can you carry all these luggages?
6 Is that luggage heavy?
7 There's a lot of rubbish in the street.
8 There's a rubbish in the hall.
9 There are lots of plastic.
10 Have you got a plastic?
11 I haven't got any money.
12 How many money have you got?
13 The news today was very interesting.
14 I heard an interesting news this morning.

Grammar: too many, too much, not enough

3 ⭐ **Complete the sentences with too much, too many, aren't enough or isn't enough.**

1 There's *too much* rubbish.
2 There _____ information.
3 There are _____ holes in the roads.
4 There _____ shops in this town.
5 There _____ good music on the radio.
6 There _____ things to do in the evenings.
7 There are _____ noisy children in this class.
8 There is _____ pollution from this factory.

4 ⭐⭐ **Complete the dialogues with one word or contraction in each space.**

A A: Why don't you like your school?
   B: I don't like it because we get
      [1]*too much* homework and we have
      [2]_____ _____ exams. There
      [3]_____ _____ holidays and there
      [4]_____ _____ free time!

B A: Why don't you play outside?
   B: There [5]_____ _____ parks
      and green spaces. I can't play in the street
      because there's [6]_____ _____
      traffic and there's [7]_____ _____
      pollution. I can't play in the garden because
      there [8]_____ _____ room – Mum
      and Dad have got [9]_____ _____
      flowers!

C A: Why don't you like holidays?
   B: We always take [10]_____ _____
      luggage. It's really heavy. We don't
      have [11]_____ money for taxis.
      Planes are always late and there
      [12]_____ _____ information
      about the flights so you wait in the airport
      for hours. At the hotel, there are always
      [13]_____ _____ old people and
      there [14]_____ never _____ children
      of my age.

Grammar: Pronouns *some-, any-, no-, every- + thing, where, one, body*

5 ⬜⭐ **Complete the sentences with the pronouns from the box.**

> • nobody • nowhere • anywhere
> • somewhere • ~~anything~~ • anyone
> • nothing • Everyone

1 Have you got _anything_ to wear to the party?

2 We've got _____ to eat. Why didn't you go shopping?

3 There's _____ to go in the evening. It's a really boring town.

4 It was great! _____ I met was really nice.

5 What a terrible party. There's _____ here.

6 I don't want to go _____ this weekend.

7 Do you know _____ who is interested in the environment?

8 Let's go _____ different this summer.

6 ⬛⭐⭐ **Complete the dialogues with the correct pronouns.**

1 A: I want to go _somewhere_ warm this summer. I want to meet _____ rich and handsome. I want to do _____ exciting.

   B: So you don't want to go camping?

2 A: Are you OK?

   B: No. I had a terrible day. _____ went wrong. I was late and the exam was difficult. I don't want to do _____ this evening. I don't want to talk to _____ and I don't want to go _____.

   A: But _____'s going to Michelle's party.

   B: No, they aren't. I'm not going.

3 A: You look upset. What's wrong?

   B: I don't want to talk about it. _____ can help me. There's _____ I can do. There's _____ I can go to escape.

   A: This sounds terrible.

   B: It is. My mum wants me to tidy my room.

Grammar summary

too many, too much, not enough

Our teachers give us **too many** tests.
There is **too much** traffic.
There **wasn't enough** information.
I think there **is enough** food now.

Note

Use

- We use *too many* with plural, countable nouns.
  There are too many people here.
- We use *too much* with uncountable nouns.
  We waste too much electricity.
- We use *(not) enough* with countable and uncountable nouns.
  There aren't enough people.
  There isn't enough money.

Pronouns *some-, any-, no-, every- + thing, where, one, body*

There's **someone/somebody** in the kitchen.
Have you got **anything** to eat?
There's **nowhere** to swim in this town.
I take my camera **everywhere** I go.

Note

Use

- We use pronouns with *some* when the identity of the person, thing or place is unknown.
  Someone picked up my bag by mistake.
- We use pronouns with *any* in questions and negative sentences.
  I didn't see anything.
- We use pronouns with *no* in positive sentences. They have the same meaning as *any* in negative sentences.
  I didn't see anything. = I saw nothing.
- We use pronouns with *every* in positive sentences to mean all the people, all the things, all the places.
  Everyone in my class forgot their homework. = All the people in my class forgot.

Common mistakes

- We don't use *no one, nobody, nothing* or *nowhere* in negative sentences.
  ~~I haven't seen no one today.~~ ✗
  I haven't seen anyone today. ✓

1   Complete the text with the words from the box.

> • art galleries   • traffic   • ~~train~~   • boat
> • underground   • parks   • expensive
> • theatre   • restaurant   • taxis   • far

Last month my parents and I went to London.
We got there by ¹_train_. At the station, lots of
²_____ were waiting so we took one to
our hotel. The hotel was quite ³_____
from the centre so we travelled everywhere by
⁴_____. There was a station near our
hotel. We had a great time. We saw a play by
Shakespeare at a ⁵_____ and we visited
lots of interesting museums and ⁶_____.
London is an ⁷_____ city, but a lot of
museums are free to visit. We ate in a great
⁸_____.
On the second day, we went along the River
Thames by ⁹_____. The only problem
with London is the ¹⁰_____. The roads are
always busy, but there are lots of ¹¹_____
with trees, flowers and grass where you can relax.
…/10

2   Choose the correct options.

I wanted to buy a stamp but ¹**somebody /
nobody** knew the way to the post office. One
man told me to ²**turn / take** the first turning on
the left. It was the wrong way. Then ³**someone /
anyone** told me to walk ⁴**along / past** the market,
but I didn't see a market ⁵**nowhere / anywhere**.
There were some tourist information ⁶**agents /
centres**, but ⁷**anything / nothing** was open. In
the end, I went back to my hotel. I was ⁸**too /
enough** tired to do anything else that day. I didn't
have ⁹**enough / too many** money to eat in the
hotel restaurant so I went to a ¹⁰**supermarket /
pharmacy** and bought a sandwich. Then I found
that they sold stamps, too. All that walking and
there were stamps for sale right next ¹¹**by / to** the
hotel! …/10

3   Cross out the incorrect word in each sentence
and write the correct one.

1 ~~Where~~ do I get to the bus station?   _How_
2 There are too much cars here.   _____
3 Buses are too slowly.   _____
4 Are this your luggage, sir?   _____
5 We haven't had nothing to
   eat yet.   _____
6 The deep of the river here is
   ten metres.   _____
7 The man in the travel agent's gave
   me some useful informations.   _____
8 There's anything good on
   TV. Let's watch a DVD.   _____
9 There is not enough bookshops
   in my town.   _____
10 How width is this bridge?   _____
11 I hated walking round Paris.
   There was too many traffic.   _____
…/10

4   Complete the text with one word in each space.

> Hi Rose,
> I'm glad you can come to my party. The best way
> to ¹_get_ to my house is by bus. The house isn't
> ²_____ from the bus station. Go out of the
> bus station and ³_____ right. Walk past the
> post ⁴_____ and then ⁵_____ the
> first turning ⁶_____ the left. My house is
> next ⁷_____Tom's Café, opposite the park.
> I've invited seven people. I wanted to ask the
> whole class, but my mum said that was too
> ⁸_____ people and that our house isn't big
> ⁹_____ to have a big party.
> Maybe she's right. With a small party, there
> won't be too ¹⁰_____ rubbish to clear up
> afterwards!
> I think that's enough information for you. Phone
> me if you need to know ¹¹_____ else.
> See you on Saturday.
> Love, Donna

…/10

🎧 **LISTEN AND CHECK YOUR SCORE**

Total	…/40

3 Skills practice

SKILLS FOCUS: READING AND WRITING

Read

1 Read the text and complete the places (1–3) with one word in each space.

1 The _____ _____

2 The _____ Museum

3 The _____ _____ Mall

> **Washington DC**, the capital of the USA, is probably best known for The White House, where the President lives. However, there is much more to see.

The Washington Monument has a height of 170 metres. It is over 100 years old and took over thirty years to build. The Monument is in The National Mall, very close to The White House.

There are nineteen museums and a zoo in the Smithsonian Museum. These include the Natural History Museum and the Museum of Air and Space. Most of the museums and the zoo are free and they are open 364 days of the year.

If you want to shop, then the place to go is the Pentagon City Mall. It has its own underground station, Pentagon City.

2 Read the text again and choose the correct options.

1 The Washington Monument is **100 / 170** metres high.

2 The Washington Monument is over **100 / 30** years old.

3 The **Washington Monument / White House** is in the National Mall.

4 The Smithsonian is **nineteen / one of nineteen** museums in Washington.

5 The zoo is **the only part / one part** of the Smithsonian which is free.

6 Pentagon City is the name of **a hotel / an underground station**.

Write

3 Look at the brochure and match the topic sentences (a–d) to the spaces (1–4).

a) Siracusa is a perfect city for walking.

b) The Piazza Duomo is the heart of the city.

c) There is no need for supermarkets in Siracusa.

d) When it's time to relax, the Italians know best.

Siracusa, Sicily's jewel

¹ _b_ You could spend your whole holiday here. However, the small lanes and roads leading off in every direction also need to be explored.

² ___ The old city, on the island of Ortygia, is small enough to be explored on foot in a day or two. Many of the streets are almost traffic free.

³ ___ Siracusa is full of cafés. The locals sit outside, watching the world go by. When you need a rest, why not do the same?

⁴ ___ For fresh food, the outdoor market is the place to go. Every day, you can find fresh fruit, vegetables, cheese and, best of all, fish from the Mediterranean Sea.

4 Write a brochure about a place that you know. Use the topic sentences to start your paragraphs.

1 The town really comes to life in the evenings.

2 There are lots of places to go to relax.

3 Use the local transport to see the town.

4 You don't need money to enjoy yourself.

4a I haven't seen the sun for weeks.

Vocabulary: Collocations with *make* and *do*

1 ⭐ **Put the phrases from the box in the correct column.**

- an appointment • some exercise
- your best • a decision
- your homework • the shopping
- a noise • friends with someone
- the housework • ~~a cake~~

Make	Do
a cake	_____
_____	_____
_____	_____
_____	_____
_____	_____

2 ⭐⭐ **Complete the sentences with the correct form of *make* or *do*.**

1 I've thought of a great way to *make* some money.

2 I've _____ you some sandwiches for your journey.

3 You're so lazy. It's midday and you haven't _____ anything yet.

4 We're _____ Physics at school this year.

5 You can have a party, but please don't _____ a mess.

6 I had a Maths test today and I _____ lots of mistakes.

7 You lay the table and I'll _____ dinner.

8 Tom is studying hard and it's _____ a difference to his marks.

Grammar: Present perfect simple with *for* and *since*

3 ⭐ **Complete the sentences with one word in each space.**

1
I've been here *since* two o'clock.
I've been here *for* two hours.
It's now *four* o'clock.

2
Mark has been in this class _____ five months.
Mark has been in this class _____ September.
It's now _____.

3
We've lived here _____ 2001.
We've lived here _____ 12 years.
It's now _____.

4
Tom has been asleep _____ nine o'clock last night.
Tom has been asleep _____ 13 hours.
It's now _____ o'clock in the morning.

5
Steve and Kathy have been together _____ two weeks.
Steve and Kathy have been together _____ 7th January.
It's now the twenty-_____ of January.

4 ★★ Use the prompts to write sentences.

1 I met Jackie three years ago.

I've known Jackie for three years. (I/know/for)

2 I bought this book last week.

_____ (I/have/for)

3 I started at this school in 2008.

_____ (I/be/since)

4 The last time I saw this film was five years ago.

_____ (I/not see/for)

5 The last time Tim was late for school was last year.

_____ (Tim/not be/since)

6 Meg arrived here thirty seconds ago.

_____ (Meg/be/for)

7 The last time my dad had a holiday was in 2010.

_____ (My dad/not have/since)

5 ★★★ Use the prompts to write questions and answers.

1 A: How long/you know/Simon?

B: I/know him/three years

A: How long have you known Simon?

B: I've known him for three years.

2 A: How long/your mum/be a teacher?

B: She/be/a teacher/1993

_____

_____

3 A: How long/you like/Justin Bieber?

B: I/like/him/last year

_____

_____

4 A: How long/you have/a dog?

B: We/have/her/about two months

_____

_____

5 A: How long/this building/be here?

B: It/be/here/2009

_____

_____

Grammar summary

Present perfect simple with *for* and *since*

Affirmative
I **have been** here **for** two hours/**since** three o'clock.
He **has lived** here **for** ten years/**since** 2003.

Negative
They **haven't seen** Paul **for** three days/**since** Tuesday.
She **hasn't watched** television **for** months/**since** before Christmas.

Questions
How long **have** you **had** that phone?
I've had it **for** two weeks/**since** my birthday.

Note

Use

- We use the Present perfect simple with *for* and *since* to talk about how long a situation that started in the past has existed.
  I have lived here for ten years. = I started living here ten years ago and I still live here now.
- We use *for* with a period of time to show how long a situation has existed.
  He's known me for a long time.
- We use *since* with a point in time to show when the situation or action started.
  She's been here since Friday.
- When we use a verb to give the point in time after *since*, we use the past simple.
  I've known him since we were young.

Common mistakes

~~We are here since 2010.~~ ✗
We've been here since 2010. ✓
~~We've known each other since three years.~~ ✗
We've known each other for three years. ✓
~~I've lived here since I have been five.~~ ✗
I've lived here since I was five. ✓

4b You've been talking for ages.

Phrases

1 ⭐ **Complete the dialogues with the words from the box.**

• tell • in • ~~ages~~ • just • about • last • on

1 A: Hurry up in the bathroom. You've been in there for *ages*.

   B: I've finished.

   A: At _____!

2 A: I can get us tickets for the concert.

   B: How? There aren't any left.

   A: Let's _____ say that I know someone who can help us.

   B: Don't _____ me. Your dad got some from work.

3 A: I'm writing an article. It's _____ bullying. Do you want to help me?

   B: OK, yes. I'm _____. I hate bullying.

   A: Great. We're _____ it!

Vocabulary: Phrasal verbs with *look*

2 ⭐ **Complete the sentences with one word in each space.**

1 Sue and Tom are looking *at* the elephant.

2 Paul is looking _____ a new word in his dictionary.

3 Sam is looking _____ to the holidays.

4 Rebecca is looking _____ her phone.

5 Sophie is looking _____ her little brother.

3 ⭐⭐ Complete the texts with the correct form of phrasal verbs with *look*.

Hi Sue,
I need to ask for your help. I agreed to [1]*look after* my neighbour's cat, but he's disappeared. I've been [2]_____ it all day.
Can you come and help me?
Thanks, **Becky x**

Hi Maria,
I'm really [3]_____ seeing you in Spain soon. I've been learning Spanish – I've been [4]_____ new words in the dictionary and [5]_____ photos of Granada. It's beautiful. I can't believe I'll be there in two weeks!
All the best, Laura x

Grammar: Present perfect continuous with *for* and *since*

4 ⭐ **Complete the sentences with the correct form of the verbs in brackets and *for* or *since*.**

1 Paul *has been watching* (watch) television *since* five o'clock.

2 I _____ (read) this book _____ three weeks.

3 You _____ (talk) on the telephone _____ ages.

4 Danny _____ (learn) Spanish _____ he was ten.

5 Lisa _____ (sing) she was a young girl.

6 It _____ (rain) hours.

7 They _____ (go) out together _____ last September.

5 ⭐⭐ Use the prompts to complete the dialogues.

1 **A:** Hi, Carol. What have you been doing this morning?

B: _I've been reading_. (I/read)

A: How long have you been reading for?

B: _____ (I/read/two hours.)

2 **A:** Steven looks tired. How long has he been swimming for?

B: _____ (He/swim/four o'clock)

A: Really? _____ (So/he/swim/two hours.) He should come out now.

B: _____ (I/tell/him to come out/half an hour.)

A: I'll tell him. Steven! Out! Now!

6 ⭐⭐⭐ Use the prompts to complete the dialogues.

1 **A:** Hello. I haven't seen you for two years. _What have you been doing since I last saw you?_ (what/you do/I last see you)

B: _____ (I cycle/around Europe)

A: For two years?

B: No, I got back last year. _____ (I work/October)

2 **A:** _____ (you/wait long?)

B: _____ (✓) _____ (I wait/45 minutes)

A: Sorry. _____ (I shop)

B: Don't worry. _____ (I watch/that boy and girl/the last ten minutes) _____ (They argue/they arrived)

A: Why?

B: I don't know. _____ (I/not listen to their conversation!)

Grammar summary

Present perfect continuous with *for* and *since*

Affirmative
I've (have) been waiting for an hour.
You**'ve (have) been working since** two o'clock.
She**'s (has) been watching** us **for** ten minutes.
He**'s (has) been playing** tennis **since** ten to one.

Negative
We **haven't been eating for** three hours.
They **haven't been crying since** last night.
He **hasn't been sleeping for** ten hours.
She **hasn't been swimming since** midday.

Questions
How long **have** you **been working?**
I've been working for two hours/**since** ten o'clock.
What **have** you **been doing** all morning?

Note

Use

- We use the present perfect continuous to talk about activities which started in the past and which are still happening now or which have very recently stopped and have a present result.
  I've been working for two hours.

- We don't use stative verbs such as *like, want, understand* with the present perfect continuous.
  I've liked history since I was young. NOT ~~I've been liking history since I was young.~~

- We can use the present perfect continuous to describe activities that aren't necessarily happening at this moment.
  She's been acting for ten years. (She may not be acting at the moment.)

Common mistakes

~~I've been knowing Simon since we were at school.~~ ✗
I've known Simon since we were at school. ✓
~~I'm waiting here for half an hour.~~ ✗
I've been waiting here for half an hour. ✓

4c She used to be a Goth.

Grammar: *used to*

1 ⭐ Complete the sentences with the correct form of the words in brackets.

1 (use/work)

   My dad _used to work_ in London, but now he works at home.

2 (use/be)

   My mum _____ a teacher, but now she works in an office.

3 (not/use/like)

   I _____ heavy metal, but now I love it.

4 (not/use/work)

   My sister _____ very hard, but now she's the best student in her class.

5 (you/use/go)

   _____ out with Melanie? Yes, but we broke up.

6 (she/use/have)

   _____ red hair? No, it was blond.

7 (use/work)

   I _____ in a restaurant on Saturdays, but now I haven't got time.

8 (your brother/use/go)

   _____ skiing? Yes, but he broke his leg.

2 ⭐⭐ Complete the text with the verbs from the box and the correct form of *used to*.

> • play (x 2) • wear • not wear • ~~ride~~
> • cycle • go • make • dream

Me and my family ten years ago
I [1]_used to ride_ my bike every day. I [2]_____
really fast! I loved my red T-shirt. I [3]_____
it all the time. My sister wore dresses all the time.
She [4]_____ trousers. She didn't like them.
She had a favourite doll. She [5]_____ with it
every day. My sister and I [6]_____ together
a lot. We [7]_____ a lot of noise, but we
were happy. We didn't have a car. Our parents
[8]_____ everywhere. I [9]_____ of
having a car, but now I cycle everywhere, too.

3 ⭐⭐⭐ Use the prompts to write questions and answers with *used to*.

1 **A:** What sports/you/use/play/when you were younger?

   A: What sports did you use to play when you
   were younger?

   B: I/use/have/tennis lessons but I/not/use/like them

   _____

2 **A:** What music/you/use/like/when you were ten?

   _____

   B: I/use/like/pop music. I not use/listen to/rock at all.

   _____

3 **A:** Where/you and your family/use/go/on holiday when you were younger?

   _____

   B: We/use/go/to Cornwall. We/not use/go abroad.

   _____

4 **A:** your/dad/use/have/long hair?

   _____

   B: No/not but my mum/use/have/pink hair!

   _____

Grammar: Echo questions

4 ⭐ Complete the echo questions with the correct verb.

1 I've been waiting for ages.   _Have_ you?

2 I haven't finished yet.   _____ you?

3 We used to live here.   _____ you?

4 Lucy doesn't want to
   come to the disco.   _____ she?

5 Gavin's late again.   _____ he?

6 They're here already.   _____ they?

7 I didn't use to like cheese.   _____ you?

8 My dad isn't going to
   help us.   _____ he?

5 ★★ Complete the dialogues with the correct echo questions.

1 **A:** I've got the computer game you told me about.

   B: *Have you*? Great!

   A: But it doesn't work.

   B: _____? Why not?

   A: I don't know.

2 **A:** My dad used to be a punk rocker.

   B: _____?

   A: Yes, and my mum was a Goth.

   B: _____? I thought she was a punk.

   A: _____? What made you think that?

3 **A:** I used to love Britney Spears.

   B: _____? I never liked her.

   A: _____? Not even when she sang *Toxic*?

   B: What?

   A: *Toxic*. It's really famous.

   B: _____? I've never heard of it.

Use your English: Show interest

6 ★★ Choose the option which is NOT possible.

1 **A:** I had a really bad day at school today.

   B: a) Did you?   b) Have you?   c) Really?

2 **A:** We're in the school's basketball final!

   B: a) How exciting! b) Are you?   c) Why not?

3 **A:** Paul doesn't want to come to my party.

   B: a) Isn't he?   b) Really?   c) Why not?

4 **A:** I need a summer job.

   B: a) Why?   b) How awful! c) Do you?

5 **A:** This used to be a park.

   B: a) Is it?   b) Really?   c) Did it?

6 **A:** My girlfriend broke up with me.

   B: a) Why?   b) Really?   c) Did you?

   A: She's met someone else.

   B: a) How awful!   b) Has she?
      c) How amazing!

Grammar summary

used to		
Affirmative		
I **used to** live in France.		
She **used to** go swimming every day.		
Negative		
He didn't **use to** listen to classical music.		
Questions		
Did she **use to** watch television all day?		
Short answers		
Yes, I **did**. No, she **didn't**.		
Wh- questions		
Where **did** they **use to** live?		

> **Note**
>
> **Use**
> - We use *used to* for past habits and states which are no longer true.
> - We can't use *used to* to talk about things which only happened once in the past.
>
> **Form**
> - The form is the same for all persons:
> - In negatives, we use *didn't* + *use* + *to* + the infinitive.
> - In questions, we use *did* + subject + *use* + *to* + the infinitive.
>
> **Common mistakes**
> ~~I didn't used to wear glasses.~~ ✗
> I didn't use to wear glasses. ✓

Echo questions	
Affirmative	
A: I'm sixteen.	B: **Are you?**
A: He likes you.	B: **Does he?**
A: We've been here before.	B: **Have you?**
Negative	
A: You aren't in the final.	B: **Aren't I?**
A: She didn't go to school yesterday.	B: **Didn't she?**
A: They can't speak French.	B: **Can't they?**

> **Note**
>
> **Use**
> - We use echo questions to show we are listening and are interested. The listener isn't asking a real question.
>
> **Form**
> - We make echo questions by using the correct auxiliary verb + the subject pronoun.
> - The negative form of *I am* is *Aren't I.*

4 Language round-up

1 Match the questions (1–7) to the answers (a–g).

1 Has she been playing tennis long? _d_

2 Why can't you go out tonight? ___

3 Did you use to play with dolls? ___

4 What are you looking for? ___

5 What is she making? ___

6 How long have you been here? ___

7 What are they doing? ___

a) My camera.   e) The ironing.

b) A cake.   f) I'm looking after my sister.

c) No, I didn't.   g) Since three o'clock.

d) Yes, she has.

.../6

2 Complete the dialogue with one word in each space.

Natalie: Hi, Sally. What's up?

Sally: I can't go to your party.

Natalie: Why ¹_not_?

Sally: Mum wants me to look ²_____ my brother.

Natalie: Oh no. We've ³_____ planning this party ⁴_____ ages.

Sally: I know. I've been really looking ⁵_____ to it.

Natalie: Can't you talk to your mum about it?

Sally: I've been talking to her ⁶_____ she told me, but I can't ⁷_____ anything about it. She says she's ⁸_____ her decision and that's it.

Natalie: Wait a minute, I've got an idea.

Sally: ⁹_____ you?

Natalie: Yes. How old is your brother?

Sally: He's twelve.

Natalie: ¹⁰_____ he? Well, you could bring him to the party.

Sally: No way.

Natalie: ¹¹_____ not? I ¹²_____ to take my little sister to parties.

Sally: ¹³_____ you?

Natalie: Yes. She loved them. Ask your mum.

.../12

3 Complete the second sentence so that it has the same meaning as the first. Use the word in capitals.

1 I've arranged a visit to get my hair cut. APPOINTMENT

I've _made an appointment_ for a haircut.

2 I never liked shopping when I was young. USE

I _____ shopping when I was young.

3 Can you take care of my dog next week? LOOK

Can you _____ when I'm on holiday?

4 I got this scarf on my birthday. HAD

I've _____ my birthday.

5 We started going out three weeks ago. BEEN

We _____ three weeks.

6 Was your sister noisy when she was a baby? BE

Did your sister _____ when she was a baby?

7 We always went for a walk in the evenings when we were in Spain. GO

We always _____ for a walk in the evenings when we were in Spain.

.../12

4 Use the prompts to write questions.

1 How long/you/wear/glasses?

How long have you been wearing glasses?

2 your sister/use/go out/on school nights?

_____

3 you/play/football/a long time?

_____

4 How long/your parents/have that car?

_____

5 How/you/use/get to primary school?

_____

6 How long/you/have/a headache?

_____

.../10

🎧 **LISTEN AND CHECK YOUR SCORE**

Total	.../40

4 Skills practice

SKILLS FOCUS: READING, LISTENING AND WRITING

Read

1 Read the text and answer true (T) or false (F).

1 The writer's grandfather has always lived in the same town. *T*

2 The air was cleaner in the past. ___

3 There aren't any factories open in the town now. ___

4 The writer's grandfather went out two evenings a week. ___

5 He didn't use to go to the cinema because of the smoke. ___

My grandfather is 73 and he's lived in this town since he was born. He's seen a lot of changes. One good thing is that the town is much cleaner now. When my grandfather was growing up, there wasn't much traffic but there were a lot of factories. On some days, the air used to be so dirty that people stayed indoors and there didn't use to be any fish in the river. Now, the factories have all gone. There is a lot of traffic and there's still some pollution, but there are more parks and the river has been clean since the 1980s.

My grandfather had a good childhood. He was a teenager when rock and roll was popular. He used to go dancing every Friday and Saturday. He didn't have much money, but everything was cheap. His family didn't have a television, but there was a cinema in the town centre. People used to smoke in the cinema! It was as polluted as the air outside, but my grandfather's parents used to take him every week when he was a boy and they used to sit in the smoky air. I can't believe he's still so healthy!

Listen

2 🎧 Listen to the conversation and answer the questions.

Who …

1 has been studying the wrong subject? *Peter*

2 is going out this evening? _____

3 doesn't like black and white films? _____

4 works better in the evening than in the morning? _____

3 🎧 Listen again and complete the sentences.

1 The two people have got a *History* exam tomorrow.

2 The Geography exam is next _____.

3 Peter goes to film club every _____.

4 Film Noir films are usually _____.

5 Peter is going to study for the exam in the _____.

6 Peter and his girlfriend had an argument because he fell asleep in the _____.

Write

4 Use the notes to complete the report about a special building.

- Name: The Shard
- Opened: 1st February 2013
- Height: 306 metres
- Floors: 72
- Designer: Renzo Piano
- Where it is: Southwark
- How to get to it: London Bridge – train or underground

¹*The Shard* is a new building in London. It opened on ² _____. It is ³ _____ high and it has ⁴ _____ floors. The designer of the building was ⁵ _____, an Italian.

I like the Shard because of its shape. It's a bit like a tall, thin, pyramid. It is made of glass and it is beautiful when the sun is shining on it.

The Shard is in ⁶ _____ in London. It is very close to ⁷ _____ railway and underground station.

5 Now write a similar description of a building in your country. Make notes first.

Notes

Notes

Notes